COMFORT FOOD RECIPE

Easy and Delicious Comfort Food Recipe Collection

(A Homemade Comfort Food Dessert Cookbook)

Mark Torres

Published by Alex Howard

© **Mark Torres**

All Rights Reserved

Comfort Food Recipe: Easy and Delicious Comfort Food Recipe Collection (A Homemade Comfort Food Dessert Cookbook)

ISBN 978-1-990169-27-4

All rights reserved. No part of this guide may be reproduced in any form without permission in writing from the publisher except in the case of brief quotations embodied in critical articles or reviews.

Legal & Disclaimer

The information contained in this book is not designed to replace or take the place of any form of medicine or professional medical advice. The information in this book has been provided for educational and entertainment purposes only.

The information contained in this book has been compiled from sources deemed reliable, and it is accurate to the best of the Author's knowledge; however, the Author cannot guarantee its accuracy and validity and cannot be held liable for any errors or omissions. Changes are periodically made to this book. You must consult your doctor or get professional medical advice before using any of the suggested remedies, techniques, or information in this book.

Table of contents

PART 1 1

1. RASPBERRY-SWIRL SWEET ROLLS 2
2. BANANA PANCAKES 5
3. APPLE FRENCH TOAST 6
4. BACON-AND-LEEK QUICHE 8
5. SPICED PUMPKIN WAFFLES 10
6. BALTHAZAR BRIOCHE FRENCH TOAST 12
7. HASH BROWNS WITH LEEKS AND BELL PEPPERS 14
8. SLOPPY JOE SLIDERS 16
9. MEATBALLS WITH GARLIC BREAD 18
10. PIGS IN A BLANKET 20
11. BAKED PASTA WITH CHICKEN SAUSAGE 22
12. SAVORY TRIPLE-CORN GRITS 24
13. HOT DOGS WITH CHEDDAR AND SAUTÉED APPLES 26
14. SKILLET CORN BREAD WITH CORN RELISH 28
15. HUSH PUPPIES WITH GREEN ZEBRA TOMATO JAM 30
16. GRILLED HAM AND CHEESE WITH PINEAPPLE 32
17. COLLARD GREENS WITH BACON 33
18. SPICED BEEF SANDWICH 34
19. FISH AND CHIPS 36
20. BRAISED LAMB SHOULDER WITH ROOT VEGETABLES 38
21. DUHALLOW CHEESE AND GRITS SOUFFLÉ 40
22. STEAK AND MUSHROOM POT PIES 41
23. THE GREATEST GRILLED CHEESE SANDWICH 43
24. SAUSAGE AND BEAN CASSEROLE 44
25. PASTITSIO 46

26. Pull-Apart Cheesy Onion Bread 48
27. Crispy French Fries 50
28. Hearty Chicken Noodle Soup 51
29. Zesty Vegetable Lasagna 52
30. Cheese Grits And Corn Pudding 54
31. Pimiento Cheese And Bacon Crostini 55
32. Herbed Potato Gratin With Roasted Garlic And Manchego 56
33. Mashed Potatoes With Crispy Shallots 58
34. Simple Shepherd's Pie 60
35. Traditional Lasagna Bolognese 61
36. Macaroni And Cheese 63
37. Fried Chicken 65
38. Chili Pot Pie With Polenta Crust 66
39. Moist Devil's Food Cake With Mrs. Milman's Chocolate Frosting............. 68
40. Peach Crisps 70
41. Ganache-Stuffed Chocolate-Chip Cookies 72
42. Brownie Sundae Cups 74
43. Brownie Coconut Ice Cream Sandwiches 76
44. S'mores Pizzas 78
45. Avocado Salsa 80
46. Classic Chicken And Dumplings 82
47. Classic Potato Latkes 83
48. Hello Yummy Bars 84
49. Mom's Pecan Pie 85
Yield: Makes 8 Servings 85
Ingredients 85
50. Caramel Cake 86
Yield: Makes 8 Servings 86

PART 2 87

Flax Seeds Vanilla Fruit Scoop 88
Spicy Nutritional Morning Diet 90
Raw Honey Strawberry Dish 92
Raw Nuts Banana Bowl 94
Carrot Orange Salad 96
Blueberry Pomegranate Salad 97
Shred Diet Berries Blend 98
Grapefruit Citrus Cream 99
Peach Cinnamon Plate 101
Blueberry Vanilla Serve 102
Almond Walnuts Morning Fillers 103
Apple Walnuts Flax Dish 105
Flax Seed Cinnamon Cakes With Berry Jam 107
Sugar Free Flax Cake With Apricot Jam 109
Nuts & Seeds Toast 111
Almond Meal Vanilla Pancakes 113
Ground Flax Seed Breakfast Burrito 115
Coconut Flour Breakfast Pizza 117
Low Carb Romaine Lettuce Salad 119
Chia Seed Dates Oatmeal 121
Spicy Almond Meal 123
Spicy Bacon With Egg Scramble 125
Egg With Pork Sausage Breakfast Skillet 127
Almond Meal Banana Pancakes 129
Cinnamon & Pumpkin With Bacon Treat 131

SALADS 133

Broccoli Salad 133

Morrocan Carrot Salad 134

Cucumber Salad 135

Chicken Salad 136

Potatoe Kugel 137

Sweet Noodle Kugel 138

Zucchini Squash Kugel 139

Apple Cranberry Kugel 140

CHICKEN 141

Schnitzel 141

Chicken In Mushroom Sauce 142

Chicken Dumplings 143

Glazed Chicken 144

MEAT 145

Peppered Roast 145

Hungarian Beef Goulash 146

Honey Brisket 147

Veal Stew 148

DESSERTS 150

Amazing Chiffon Cake 150

Flaky Apricot Rugelach 151

Chocolate Mousse Cake 152

Spiced Coffee Cake 153

Low Carb Zucchini Tomato Salad 154

Easy Tomato Bisque 155

Spicy Kelp Noodle Salsa & Cashew Sauce 156

Raw Almond & Paprika 158

Sweet Cabbage Avocado Slaw 159

Pink Fresh Coconut Shake 160
Celery With Pitted Dates 161
Vanilla Blueberry Energy Bars 162
Sweet Vanilla Peaches 163
Raw Hazelnut Fudge 164
Ginger Apricot Cookies 165
Cauliflower Shrimp Mussels 166
Easy Vanilla Chocó Soufflé 168
Eggs With Smoked Salmon 170
Pink Chia Creamy Bread 172
Almond With Apple Sauce – A Low Carb Morning Dish 174
No Grain Low Carb Almond Bread 176
Low Carb Almond Corn Muffins 178
Quick Delicious Almond Biscuits – Evening Snack 180
Coconut & Almond Flour Fry Bread 181
Crunchy Coconut Crackers 183
Chocó Dip With Celery 185
Chocó Pecan Snack 186
Vanilla Chocó Chip Cookies 187
Sugar-Free Coconut Ice Cream 188

Part 1

1. Raspberry-Swirl Sweet Rolls

TOTAL TIME: 4:30
COOK: 0:30
LEVEL: MODERATE
YIELD: 16 ROLLS

INGREDIENTS
Dough

- 1 c. milk
- 0.67 c. sugar
- 1.50 tbsp. active dry yeast
- 1 stick unsalted butter
- 2 large eggs
- 1 tsp. lemon zest
- 0.50 tsp. fine sea salt
- 4.25 c. all-purpose flour
- all-purpose flour

Filling

- 1 package IQF (Individually Quick Frozen) raspberries
- 0.25 c. sugar
- 2 tbsp. sugar
- 1 tsp. cornstarch

Glaze

- 0.75 c. confectioners' sugar
- 3 tbsp. unsalted butter
- 1.50 tbsp. heavy cream

DIRECTIONS

1. Make the Dough: In a small saucepan, warm the milk over moderately low heat until it's 95 degrees F. Pour the warm milk into the bowl of a standing electric mixer fitted with the dough hook and stir in the sugar and yeast. Let stand until the yeast is foamy, about 5 minutes. Add the softened butter, eggs, grated lemon zest, and sea salt. Add the flour and beat at medium speed until a soft dough forms, about 3 minutes. Increase the speed to medium-high and beat until the dough is soft and supple, about 10 minutes longer.
2. Scrape the dough out onto a lightly floured surface and knead it with your hands 2 or 3 times. Form the dough into a ball and transfer it to a lightly buttered bowl. Cover the dough with plastic wrap and let stand in a warm place until doubled in bulk, 1 to 2 hours.
3. Line the bottom of a 9- by 13-inch baking pan with parchment paper, allowing the paper to extend up the short sides. Butter the paper and sides of the pan. Turn the dough out onto a lightly floured work surface and, using a rolling pin, roll it into a 10- by 24-inch rectangle.
4. Make the Filling: In a medium bowl, toss the frozen raspberries with the sugar and cornstarch. Spread the raspberry filling evenly over the dough. Tightly roll up the dough to form a 24-inch-long log. Working quickly, cut the log into quarters. Cut each quarter into 4 slices and arrange them in the baking pan, cut sides up. Scrape any berries and juice from the work surface into the baking pan between the rolls. Cover the rolls and let them rise in a warm place until they are puffy and have filled the baking pan, about 2 hours.
5. Preheat the oven to 425 degrees F. Bake the rolls for about 25 minutes, until they are golden and the berries are bubbling. Transfer the pan to a rack to cool for 30 minutes.
6. Meanwhile, Make the Glaze: In a small bowl, whisk the confectioners' sugar with the butter and heavy cream until the glaze is thick and spreadable.

7. Invert the rolls onto the rack and peel off the parchment paper. Invert the rolls onto a platter. Dollop glaze over each roll and spread with an offset spatula. Serve warm or at room temperature.

2. Banana Pancakes

LEVEL: MODERATE
YIELD: 1 1/2 DOZEN

INGREDIENTS

- 1 c. all-purpose flour
- 2 tbsp. sugar
- 2 tsp. baking powder
- 0.50 tsp. salt
- 1 large egg
- 1 c. milk
- 2 tbsp. unsalted butter
- 2 bananas

DIRECTIONS

1. Preheat oven to 175 degrees F. Whisk flour, sugar, baking powder, and salt in a medium bowl. Add egg, milk, and butter; whisk until combined but still slightly lumpy.
2. Heat a large nonstick skillet over medium heat. Place 5 banana rounds in pan, about 3 inches apart. Spoon one tablespoon batter over each; cook until large bubbles cover surface, 1 to 2 minutes. Flip, and cook until bottom is golden, about 1 minute more. Transfer to a baking sheet, and keep warm in the oven.
3. Repeat with remaining banana rounds and batter. Saute extra banana slices in butter until golden; serve with pancakes.

3. Apple French Toast

TOTAL TIME: 0:55
PREP: 0:30
LEVEL: MODERATE
SERVES: 6

INGREDIENTS
- 2 tbsp. unsalted butter
- 4 large crisp-sweet apples (such as Jonamac or Empire)
- 0.75 tsp. nutmeg
- 0.25 c. granulated sugar
- 1 loaf challah
- 3 large eggs
- 0.50 c. milk
- 0.25 tsp. cinnamon
- 0.13 tsp. salt
- confectioners' sugar

DIRECTIONS

1. In a large skillet over medium heat, melt butter. Add apples and 1/4 teaspoon nutmeg and cook until apples begin to brown, about 5 minutes. Add 2 tablespoons water and granulated sugar; stir to coat apples. Cook until fruit is tender, about 5 more minutes, then set aside.
2. Heat a griddle or large skillet over medium heat. Heat oven to 350 degrees F. Fit a baking pan with a wire rack; set aside.
3. Make a 2-inch slit into each bread slice to create a pocket. Stuff about 3 tablespoons apple mixture into each bread pocket; press to close. In a large, shallow bowl, whisk together eggs, milk, cinnamon, salt and remaining 1/2 teaspoon nutmeg.
4. Brush griddle with butter. Dip bread slices into egg mixture; cook until golden, about 2 minutes per side. Transfer to

prepared baking pan; bake batch until heated through, 12 to 15 minutes. Sprinkle with confectioners' sugar.

4. Bacon-And-Leek Quiche

TOTAL TIME: 2:30
COOK: 0:30
LEVEL: MODERATE
YIELD: MAKES TWO 10-INCH TARTS

INGREDIENTS
- 2.50 c. all-purpose flour
- 0.50 tsp. salt
- 1.50 stick cold unsalted butter
- 1 large egg yolk
- 0.25 c. ice water
- 3 tbsp. ice water
- 1 lb. thickly sliced bacon
- 3 large leeks
- 1 tsp. chopped thyme leaves
- Salt and freshly ground white pepper
- 8 oz. cave-aged Gruyère cheese
- 4 large eggs
- 2 large egg yolks
- 2.50 c. heavy cream or half-and-half

DIRECTIONS
1. Make the crust: In a food processor, pulse the 2 1/2 cups of flour with the salt. Add the butter and pulse until it is the size of small peas. Add the egg yolk and ice water and pulse until the pastry is moistened. Turn the pastry out onto a floured work surface and knead 2 or 3 times, just until smooth. Pat the pastry into 2 disks, wrap in plastic, and refrigerate until firm, about 20 minutes.
2. Preheat the oven to 375 degrees. On a floured surface, roll 1 disk of the pastry to a 12-inch round. Ease the pastry into a 10-inch fluted tart pan with a removable bottom without stretching. Trim the excess and use it to patch any holes. Refrigerate the tart shell for 10 minutes. Repeat with the remaining pastry.
3. Line the tart shells with foil and fill with pie weights or dried beans. Bake the tart shells for 30 minutes, just until dry. Remove the foil and pie weights and bake the crusts for about 15 minutes longer, until they are dry and golden. Transfer the tart pans to 2 sturdy baking sheets.
4. Meanwhile, make the filling: In a large skillet, cook the bacon over moderately high heat, stirring, until browned and crisp, about 7 minutes. Drain the bacon, leaving 1 tablespoon of the fat in the pan. Add the leeks and thyme to the skillet, season with salt and white pepper, and cook over moderate heat, stirring occasionally, until the leeks are softened but not browned, about 5 minutes. Transfer to a bowl and let cool. Stir in the bacon and cheese.
5. Divide the bacon-and-leek filling between the tart shells. In a bowl, whisk the eggs with the egg yolks and heavy cream. Season lightly with salt and white pepper. Pour the custard into the tart shells and bake for about 30 minutes, rotating the sheet halfway through for even baking, until puffed and lightly browned. Transfer the quiches to a rack and let cool for 15 minutes. Remove the rings, cut the quiches into wedges, and serve.

5. Spiced Pumpkin Waffles

LEVEL: MODERATE

SERVES: 8

INGREDIENTS

- 2.50 c. all-purpose flour
- 1 tbsp. baking powder
- 2 tsp. cinnamon
- 1 tsp. ginger
- 0.50 tsp. baking soda
- 0.50 tsp. salt
- 0.50 tsp. fresh-ground nutmeg
- 0.25 tsp. cloves
- 4 large eggs
- 2 c. buttermilk
- 1 c. pumpkin purée
- 0.50 c. dark brown sugar
- 0.25 c. unsalted butter
- 1 tsp. pure vanilla extract

DIRECTIONS

1. Preheat a waffle iron. Combine the flour, baking powder, cinnamon, ginger, baking soda, salt, nutmeg, and cloves in a large bowl and set aside.

2. Whisk together the eggs, buttermilk, pumpkin purée, sugar, butter, and vanilla in another large bowl until smooth. While whisking, add the flour mixture and blend until smooth.

3. Generously coat the waffle iron with vegetable oil and cook the batter in the waffle iron as recommended in the manufacturer's instructions. Repeat with remaining batter.

6. Balthazar Brioche French Toast

LEVEL: MODERATE
YIELD: 4 TO 6 SERVINGS
SERVES: 4

INGREDIENTS
- 6 large eggs
- 0.50 c. superfine sugar
- 4 c. milk
- 1 tsp. ground cinnamon
- 1 pinch nutmeg
- 1 loaf day-old brioche or challah bread
- 0.25 c. Clarified Butter
- 2 tbsp. unsalted butter
- confectioners' sugar
- **Syrup**
- Fresh fruit or crisp cooked bacon

DIRECTIONS
1. In a large bowl, whisk together eggs, sugar, and milk. Add cinnamon and nutmeg; whisk to combine.
2. Layer bread slices in a shallow baking dish and pour over egg mixture; let stand until bread begins to absorb liquid, 2 to 3 minutes. Turn bread slices and let bread absorb liquid on the opposite side, 2 to 3 minutes more.
3. Preheat oven to 200 degrees F. Place a baking sheet or ovenproof serving platter in oven.
4. Working in batches, coat the bottom of a medium skillet with some of the clarified butter and heat over medium-high heat. Add 3 to 4 slices of soaked bread and cook until golden brown and crisp. Turn bread and cook until golden brown and crisp, adding butter as necessary to help browning and to give the

French toast a nutty flavor. Transfer French toast to baking sheet in oven to keep warm. Repeat process with remaining clarified butter, soaked bread, and butter.

5. Serve French toast immediately dusted with confectioners' sugar, syrup, and fresh fruit or bacon, if desired.

7. Hash Browns With Leeks And Bell Peppers

LEVEL: EASY

SERVES: 8

INGREDIENTS

- 2 tbsp. extra-virgin olive oil
- 2 medium leeks
- 0.50 bell pepper (green or red)
- 1.50 tsp. salt
- 0.50 tsp. Freshly ground black pepper
- 2 lb. russet potatoes
- 2 tsp. thyme
- 1 tbsp. butter

DIRECTIONS

1. Heat 1 tablespoon olive oil in a 10" nonstick skillet over medium heat. Add leeks and bell pepper; season to taste with salt and pepper. Cook, stirring occasionally, until softened and just golden, 6 to 8 minutes. Transfer to a large bowl and set aside; rinse and dry skillet.

2. Meanwhile, grate potatoes on large holes of a box grater. Working quickly (they discolor after grating) with a small handful at a time, firmly squeeze potatoes to remove as much liquid as possible (it's important for the grated potatoes to be as dry as possible before cooking to prevent them from sticking to the skillet); discard liquid and transfer potatoes to bowl with leek mixture.

3. Add thyme, 1 1/2 teaspoon salt, and 1/2 teaspoon pepper to mixture; toss well.

4. Heat 1/2 tablespoon butter and 1/2 tablespoon olive oil in skillet over medium heat. Add potato mixture; press down firmly with a rubber spatula to form a potato cake. Tidy the edges, then cook, gently shaking skillet from time to time to prevent sticking, until cake is a deep golden brown, 8 to 10 minutes.

5. Loosen edges, then gently slide hash browns onto a large plate. While heating remaining butter and olive oil in skillet, place a second plate on top of hash browns and flip (so cooked side will face up). Glide inverted cake back into the warmed skillet and cook until deep golden brown on second side, 8 to 10 minutes. Slide hash browns onto a platter. Cool for 5 minutes, then cut into wedges and serve.

8. Sloppy Joe Sliders

TOTAL TIME: 0:30
PREP: 0:15
LEVEL: MODERATE
SERVES: 8

INGREDIENTS
- 1.00 tbsp. olive oil
- 1.00 large onion
- 2.00 clove garlic
- Coarse salt and ground pepper
- 0.75 lb. ground beef sirloin
- 1.00 can tomato puree
- 0.50 tsp. mustard powder
- 1.50 tsp. dark-brown sugar
- 1.00 tbsp. cider vinegar
- 16.00 party-size potato rolls

DIRECTIONS

1. Heat oil over medium in a large saucepan. Add onion and garlic; season with salt and pepper. Cook until softened, stirring occasionally, 6 to 8 minutes.

2. Add beef, and cook, breaking up meat with a wooden spoon, until no longer pink, 4 to 5 minutes. Add tomato puree, mustard powder, sugar, and vinegar. Cook, stirring occasionally, until slightly thickened, 8 to 10 minutes. (To store, refrigerate, up to 2 days.) Serve warm on rolls.

9. Meatballs With Garlic Bread

TOTAL TIME: 0:35
PREP: 0:25
LEVEL: MODERATE
SERVES: 4

INGREDIENTS

- 3 hoagie rolls
- 1 lb. ground beef chuck
- 1 large egg
- 3 tsp. minced garlic
- Coarse salt
- ground pepper
- 0.75 tsp. dried oregano
- 2 tbsp. extra-virgin olive oil
- 1 tsp. extra-virgin olive oil
- 1 can crushed tomatoes
- 1 can whole peeled tomatoes
- sugar

DIRECTIONS

1. Preheat oven to 400 degrees. Tear 1 roll into pieces; pulse in a food processor until fine crumbs form. In a large bowl, toss crumbs with 1/3 cup water. Add beef, egg, 1 teaspoon garlic, 2 teaspoons salt, 1/4 teaspoon pepper, and 1/2 teaspoon oregano; mix just until combined. Gently form mixture into 12 meatballs.

2. In a large Dutch oven or heavy pot, heat 1 teaspoon oil over medium-high; swirl to coat. Add meatballs and cook, turning occasionally, until browned, about 7 minutes.

3. Add crushed and whole tomatoes with juice (breaking up tomatoes), 1 teaspoon garlic, teaspoon oregano, and pinch of sugar. Season with salt and pepper. Bring sauce to a boil; reduce to a rapid simmer and cook until meatballs are cooked through, about 15 minutes.

4. Meanwhile, split 2 rolls and place, cut side up, on a rimmed baking sheet. Brush with 2 tablespoons oil and sprinkle with 1 teaspoon garlic; season with salt and pepper. Bake until golden, about 10 minutes. Serve meatballs with garlic bread.

10. Pigs In A Blanket

LEVEL: MODERATE

YIELD: 2 DOZEN

INGREDIENTS

- 2 tbsp. butter
- 1 large yellow onion
- 0.50 tsp. kosher salt
- 0.25 tsp. Black pepper
- **1 egg**
- 1 frozen all-butter puff pastry dough
- 4 pork hot dogs or beef hot dogs
- Chinese hot mustard

DIRECTIONS

1. Preheat oven to 375 degrees. Melt butter in a large skillet over medium heat. Add onion and cook, stirring occasionally, until soft and golden brown, 10 to 12 minutes; stir in salt and pepper. Cool, then finely chop and set aside.

2. In a small bowl, whisk together 1 tablespoon water and egg to make an egg wash; set aside. Arrange puff pastry on a clean surface and cut into 24 triangles, each about 2 inches wide at the bottom and about 3 inches tall. Transfer to a sheet tray, cover with plastic wrap, and keep refrigerated while working on step 3.

3. Remove a few pieces of puff pastry from refrigerator at a time, so that the rest remain chilled until ready to use. Spoon about 2 teaspoons onion onto a 3-inch end of each puff pastry triangle, then top with a piece of hot dog. Roll up, starting with hot dog end first. Along the way, using your fingers or a pastry brush, dab the puff pastry with a bit of egg wash to help seal. Transfer to a parchment-paper-lined baking sheet, seam side down.

4. Brush pigs in a blanket thinly with some of the egg wash and bake until puffed and golden brown, about 25 minutes. Transfer to a platter and serve with mustard.

11. Baked Pasta With Chicken Sausage

TOTAL TIME: 1:15
PREP: 0:30
LEVEL: MODERATE
SERVES: 8

INGREDIENTS
- Coarse salt and ground pepper
- 1 tbsp. olive oil
- 1 medium red onion
- 4 clove garlic
- 0.25 c. vodka (optional)
- 1 can whole tomatoes with juice
- 0.50 tsp. dried oregano
- 0.50 c. heavy cream
- 1 lb. rigatoni
- 10 oz. baby spinach
- 12 oz. smoked chicken sausage
- 6 oz. Fontina cheese
- 0.25 c. grated Parmesan cheese

DIRECTIONS

1. Bring a large pot of salted water to a boil. Heat oil in a large skillet over medium heat. Add onion; cook until translucent, about 3 minutes. Stir in garlic. Remove from heat; add vodka, if desired. Return to heat; cook until almost evaporated, 1 minute.

2. Stir in tomatoes and oregano; cook until tomatoes are falling apart, 10 to 15 minutes. Add cream; cook until warmed through, about 5 minutes. Season sauce with salt and pepper.

3. Meanwhile, preheat oven to 400 degrees F. Cook pasta in the boiling water until al dente, according to package instructions. Add spinach, and cook just until wilted. Drain, and return contents to pot.

4. Add tomato sauce, sausage, and cubed fontina to pot; toss to coat. Season with salt and pepper. Divide evenly between two shallow 1 1/2-quart baking dishes.

5. Top with grated fontina and Parmesan. Bake until browned and edges are crisp, 20 to 30 minutes.

12. Savory Triple-Corn Grits

LEVEL: MODERATE
YIELD: 4 TO 6 SERVINGS
SERVES: 4

INGREDIENTS
- 0.50 c. raw cashews
- 1.25 tsp. fine sea salt
- 2 ear fresh sweet corn
- 2 tbsp. extra-virgin olive oil
- 1 large yellow onion
- 1 tsp. ground cumin
- 2 clove garlic
- 0.50 c. cornmeal
- 0.50 c. stone-ground grits
- freshly ground white pepper

DIRECTIONS
1. Soak cashews in water overnight; drain. In a blender, combine cashews, 1/4 teaspoon salt, and 1/4 cup water; blend until smooth. Set aside.
2. Bring a small pot of salted water to a boil. Turn off heat, add corn kernels, and let sit for 1 minute. Drain and set aside.
3. In a medium sauté pan over medium heat, warm the oil; add onion, cumin, and 1/2 teaspoon salt. Cook, stirring occasionally, until softened, about 7 minutes. Add garlic and cook until softened, about 2 minutes more. Set aside half of onion mixture in a small bowl. Add reserved corn to pan and cook for an additional 2 minutes. Set aside.
4. In a bowl, mix cornmeal and grits well. In a medium saucepan, combine 3 cups water and 1/2 teaspoon salt and bring to a boil. Slowly whisk in cornmeal and grits until no lumps remain, return to a boil, then quickly reduce heat to low. Simmer, stirring occasionally to prevent grits from sticking to bottom of pan, until grits have absorbed most of the liquid and are thickening, about 3 minutes. Stir in 1 cup water and simmer 10 minutes more, stirring occasionally, until most of the liquid has been absorbed. Stir in creamed cashews and corn-onion mixture. Cover and simmer, stirring frequently, until grits are soft and fluffy, about 30 minutes.
5. Season with salt and white pepper to taste. Garnish with onion mixture.

13. Hot Dogs With Cheddar And Sautéed Apples

TOTAL TIME: 0:45

LEVEL: MODERATE

SERVES: 6

INGREDIENTS

- 2 tbsp. unsalted butter
- 3 large peeled Granny Smith apples
- 3 tbsp. light brown sugar
- 1 pinch cinnamon
- 6 hot dogs
- 6 long pretzel rolls or hot dog buns
- 3 oz. sharp Cheddar cheese

DIRECTIONS

1. Preheat the oven to 450 degrees F. In a large skillet, melt the butter. Add the apples and cook over moderate heat, stirring occasionally, until barely softened and just beginning to brown, about 5 minutes. Add the brown sugar and cook over moderately low heat, stirring occasionally, until the apples are tender and lightly caramelized, about 10 minutes longer. Stir in the cinnamon and keep warm.

2. Heat a grill pan. Grill the hot dogs over high heat until lightly charred all over, about 5 minutes. On a baking sheet, set the dogs in the rolls and top with the cheddar cheese. Bake for about 3 minutes, just until the cheese is melted. Top with the apples and serve at once.

14. Skillet Corn Bread With Corn Relish

TOTAL TIME: 1:00

COOK: 0:35

LEVEL: MODERATE

YIELD: ONE 10-INCH ROUND CORN BREAD

INGREDIENTS

- 1 stick unsalted butter
- 1.50 c. all-purpose flour
- 0.75 c. stone-ground yellow or white cornmeal
- 1 tbsp. baking powder
- 1 tbsp. sugar
- 2 tsp. kosher salt
- 2 large eggs
- 1.25 c. milk
- 1.50 c. well-drained Corn Relish with Roasted Peppers

DIRECTIONS

1. Preheat the oven to 425 degrees F. Heat a 10-inch cast-iron skillet over low heat and add 2 tablespoons of the butter.

2. In a large bowl, whisk the flour with the cornmeal, baking powder, sugar, and salt. In a large glass measuring cup, melt the remaining 6 tablespoons of butter in a microwave oven. Whisk in the eggs and milk until blended. Add the liquid ingredients and the Corn Relish to the cornmeal mixture and stir with a spatula just until the batter is evenly moistened.

3. Scrape the batter into the hot skillet and spread it evenly. Bake in the center of the oven for about 35 minutes, until the corn bread is golden and a toothpick inserted into the center comes out clean. Transfer the skillet to a rack and let the corn bread cool for about 20 minutes. Cut into squares and serve.

15. Hush Puppies With Green Zebra Tomato Jam

TOTAL TIME: 1:40
COOK: 0:40
LEVEL: MODERATE
YIELD: ABOUT 3 1/2 DOZEN

INGREDIENTS
- 1 c. yellow cornmeal
- 1 c. all-purpose flour
- 3 tbsp. sugar
- 1 tbsp. kosher salt
- 1 tbsp. baking powder
- 1 large egg
- 1 c. milk
- 3 tbsp. unsalted butter
- 2 lb. Green Zebra tomatoes
- 0.50 c. honey
- 0.50 c. apple cider vinegar
- 0.25 c. sugar
- 1 tbsp. finely grated fresh ginger
- 1 clove garlic
- 1 cinnamon stick
- 1.50 tsp. ground cumin
- 0.25 tsp. cayenne pepper
- **salt**
- vegetable oil

DIRECTIONS

1. Prepare the hush puppies: In a large bowl, whisk the cornmeal with the flour, sugar, salt, and baking powder. Add the egg, milk, and melted butter. Whisk until smooth. Cover and refrigerate the hush puppy batter for at least 1 hour.

2. Meanwhile, make the jam: In a medium saucepan, combine the diced tomatoes with the honey, vinegar, sugar, ginger, garlic, cinnamon stick, cumin, and cayenne. Bring to a boil and simmer over moderately low heat, stirring occasionally, until thick and jammy, about 40 minutes. Discard the cinnamon stick. Season the tomato jam with salt. Transfer the jam to a bowl and let cool.

3. Preheat the oven to 400 degrees F. In a large saucepan, heat 2 inches of oil to 350 degrees F. Set a rack over a large rimmed baking sheet and place near the stove. Stir the hush puppy batter. Drop tablespoon-size balls of batter into the hot oil, about 6 at a time, and fry, turning a few times, until they're deeply browned and cooked through, about 3 minutes. With a slotted spoon, transfer the hush puppies to the rack to drain. Repeat with the remaining batter. When all of the hush puppies have been fried, reheat them in the oven for about 3 minutes, or until they're hot. Serve them with the green tomato jam.

16. Grilled Ham And Cheese With Pineapple

TOTAL TIME: 0:15
PREP: 0:10
LEVEL: EASY
SERVES: 1

INGREDIENTS
- 2 slice sandwich bread
- 2 slice Swiss cheese
- 2.00 oz. thinly sliced ham
- 2.00 thin rounds pineapple
- 3.00 fresh basil leaves
- 1.00 tbsp. butter

DIRECTIONS

1. Layer 1 slice sandwich bread with 1 slice Swiss cheese, ham, pineapple, fresh basil, and another slice of cheese; top with bread.
2. In a skillet over medium-low, melt butter. Add sandwich. Cover; cook until golden, 2 to 3 minutes.
3. Flip; cook, covered, until cheese is melted.

17. Collard Greens With Bacon

LEVEL: EASY

INGREDIENTS
- 2.00 bunch collard greens
- 2.00 tsp. vegetable oil
- 0.50 red onion
- 3.00 slice bacon
- 2.00 tbsp. cider vinegar

DIRECTIONS
1. Working in batches, stack greens; cut crosswise into 2-inch-thick strips. Gather strips; cut crosswise into 2-inch pieces. Transfer to a large bowl of cold water; swish to remove grit. Transfer greens to a colander using a slotted spoon; let drain. Repeat until greens are free of grit.
2. Heat oil in a very large skillet over medium-high heat. Add onion and bacon; cook until onions are translucent, about 4 minutes. Add greens; cook, stirring, until greens begin to wilt and are reduced in volume.
3. Raise heat to high; add vinegar. Cook, scraping up brown bits from bottom of skillet, until vinegar has evaporated, about 1 minute.
4. Add stock; reduce heat. Simmer, covered, until greens are just tender, 12 to 14 minutes. If making ahead, refrigerate, covered; reheat over low heat.

18. Spiced Beef Sandwich

TOTAL TIME: 7:00
COOK: 7:00
LEVEL: MODERATE
SERVES: 10

INGREDIENTS
- 1 tsp. ground cloves
- 1 tsp. ground pepper
- 1 tsp. ground allspice
- 1 tsp. ground cinnamon
- 1 tsp. ground nutmeg
- 1 tbsp. brown sugar
- 0.25 c. kosher salt
- 1 tbsp. molasses
- 4 lb. boneless tied beef rib roast or chuck roast
- 12 oz. Guinness Stout
- **Bread**
- bottled horseradish
- **Coleslaw**
- Pickles

DIRECTIONS

1. Mix spices, sugar, and salt in a bowl. Stir in molasses to form a dry paste; rub all over beef. Place meat in a nonreactive container or resealable bag. Let marinate 4 to 7 days in the refrigerator, turning and rubbing beef once each day.

2. Place beef and stout in a wide (6- to 8-quart) pot and add water to just cover beef. Bring to a simmer; cover and cook until tender but not falling apart, about 3 hours (30 minutes more if using chuck). Remove from heat, but let beef sit in pot for 2 hours. When cool, remove beef and chill in refrigerator at least 2 hours.

3. Slice meat and assemble sandwiches with bread; if desired, add horseradish to taste. Serve with coleslaw and pickles.

19. Fish And Chips

LEVEL: MODERATE
SERVES: 4
INGREDIENTS
- 2 c. all-purpose flour
- 1 tsp. baking powder
- 0.50 tsp. salt
- 1 tsp. malt vinegar
- 1 gal. canola oil
- 2 lb. russet potatoes
- 4 cod fillets

DIRECTIONS

1. Combine flour, baking powder, and salt in a mixing bowl. Whisk in 1 3/4 cups water and stir in vinegar; set batter aside.

2. Heat canola oil to 300 degrees; in a deep fryer or a deep, heavy pot with a candy thermometer. Peel and cut potatoes lengthwise to form long, 1/4-inch-thick "chips." Add to oil, and fry 10 minutes, stirring occasionally. Remove and drain well on paper towels, then place in refrigerator to chill, 10 to 15 minutes. Keep oil in pot on stove, but turn off heat.

3. Bring oil to 350 degrees. Fry chips a second time, in two batches, until golden brown and crisp, 2 to 3 minutes per batch. Drain well on clean paper towels. (Keep chips warm in a 250 degree oven while cooking fish.)

4. Dip 2 cod fillets in reserved batter and slowly ease them into oil. Fry until golden brown and cooked through, about 7 minutes; drain well on paper towels. Repeat with last 2 fillets. Serve hot with extra salt and vinegar on the side.

20. Braised Lamb Shoulder With Root Vegetables

LEVEL: MODERATE

SERVES: 8

INGREDIENTS

- 1 lamb shoulder
- **salt**
- **Pepper**
- 1 tbsp. canola oil
- 1 head garlic
- 2 celery stalks
- 3 carrots
- 1 onion
- 4 sprig thyme
- 4 sprig rosemary
- 1 bay leaf
- 6 c. lamb stock or beef stock
- 8 baby carrots
- 8 baby turnips
- 8 baby parsnips
- 4.50 tsp. sugar
- 1 tsp. unsalted butter

DIRECTIONS

1. Preheat oven to 275 degrees F. Season lamb with 1 tablespoon salt and 1 teaspoon pepper. Heat a roasting pan across 2 burners; add oil and sear lamb on all sides. Place garlic, celery, carrots, onion, and herbs in pan; add stock. Bring to a simmer. Cover tightly with foil and braise in oven 3 hours, or until tender but not falling off bone.

2. Meanwhile, peel and coarsely chop root vegetables. Place baby carrots in a small pot, cover with water, and add sugar and 1 1/2 teaspoon salt. Bring to a simmer and cook until tender when pierced with a knife. Remove with a slotted spoon (keeping water on stove), and place carrots in a colander; run under cold water to cool, and set aside. Repeat process, first with turnips, then with parsnips. Chill cooked root vegetables until ready to serve.

3. Remove foil and allow lamb to cool in its liquid. When cool, remove bones and divide meat into 6 to 8 portions. Strain braising liquid, and reduce sauce in a medium pan over medium heat for 20 minutes. Add salt and pepper to taste, and gently heat lamb in pan. In a small sautè pan, warm root vegetables with butter; season to taste with salt and pepper. To serve, divide lamb and vegetables among plates. Pour sauce over each.

21. Duhallow Cheese And Grits Soufflé

LEVEL: MODERATE

SERVES: 8

INGREDIENTS

- 2.50 c. whole milk
- 1 c. coarse white grits
- 8 tbsp. unsalted butter
- 3 c. Duhallow or mild Cheddar cheese
- **salt**
- **Pepper**
- 4 large eggs

DIRECTIONS

1. Add milk and 2 1/2 cups water to a heavy, medium saucepan; bring to a boil over medium heat. Whisk in grits, and simmer 10 minutes, stirring constantly. Reduce heat to the lowest setting possible; cover and cook until grits are creamy and tender, stirring frequently, about 1 hour (time will vary depending on grits; add hot water if they are getting too thick).
2. Preheat oven to 350 degrees F. Transfer grits to a large bowl and cool slightly. Stir in butter and cheese; season to taste with salt and pepper. Stir in egg yolks.
3. Using an electric mixer, beat egg whites with a pinch of salt to stiff peaks. Fold into grits. Transfer to a large buttered ovenproof dish and bake until golden, about 45 minutes. Serve immediately.

22. Steak And Mushroom Pot Pies

TOTAL TIME: 0:44
PREP: 0:20
COOK: 0:24
LEVEL: MODERATE
SERVES: 4

INGREDIENTS
- 1 sheet frozen puff pastry
- 2 tbsp. olive oil
- 1 lb. beef fillet
- 0.75 lb. mixed mushrooms
- 1 large onion
- 1 tbsp. chopped fresh rosemary
- 1 tbsp. tomato paste
- 2 clove garlic
- 2 tbsp. flour
- 1.50 c. reduced-sodium beef stock or broth
- 1 c. frozen peas and carrots
- 0.50 tsp. kosher salt
- 0.50 tsp. Freshly ground pepper
- 1 large egg

DIRECTIONS

1. Heat oven to 400 degrees F. Place 4 deep crocks or ramekins (1 1/4-cup capacity) on a baking sheet. Unfold pastry on a lightly floured surface; roll out seams in dough with a rolling pin. Cut dough into 4 pieces; trim each piece to fit over tops of crocks with an additional 1/2-inch on each side. Place dough on a waxed-paper-lined plate and refrigerate.

2. Heat 1 tablespoon of the oil in a large nonstick skillet over high heat until oil is shimmering. Sauté beef, in 2 batches, 1 1/2 minutes per batch, until lightly browned. Transfer to a plate. Add remaining 1 tablespoon oil to skillet with mushrooms and onions; sauté over medium-high heat 4 minutes until mushrooms are softened and onions are translucent.

3. Stir in rosemary, tomato paste, and garlic, then sprinkle flour over mixture; stir for 1 minute. Add stock, bring to a boil, and cook until thickened, about 3 minutes. Stir in peas and carrots, salt, and pepper, then beef cubes.

4. Spoon mixture into crocks. Brush outside edges of crocks lightly with egg wash. Place pastry cut-outs over top of crocks and press dough overhang against outside edges of crocks to adhere. Cut vent holes in centers; brush pastry with egg wash. Bake 24 minutes or until pastry is golden and puffed.

23. The Greatest Grilled Cheese Sandwich

LEVEL: EASY

SERVES: 6

INGREDIENTS

- 12 slice challah or brioche
- 6 tbsp. butter
- 12 oz. Shredded cheese

DIRECTIONS

1. Optional additional toppings:
2. Grilled onions and bacon
3. Grainy mustard and sliced tomato
4. Smoked ham and roasted peppers
5. Butter one side of each slice of bread.
6. Heat a flat griddle or large frying pan over medium heat. Mound about 1/2 cup (2 ounces) cheese on each of 6 slices of bread (unbuttered side). Add any optional toppings (if using). Place remaining bread on top, buttered side up. Place 1 or 2 sandwiches (do not crowd) on griddle or skillet. (Don't let griddle get too hot or bread will brown before cheese is melted.) When bread is golden brown underneath, turn sandwiches over and press flat with a spatula. Reduce heat to medium-low and continue cooking until cheese is melted and bread is golden brown on both sides. Repeat with remaining bread and cheese. Slice and serve hot.

24. Sausage And Bean Casserole

TOTAL TIME: 1:15

PREP: 0:45

LEVEL: MODERATE

SERVES: 8

INGREDIENTS
- 12.00 slice white sandwich bread
- Coarse salt
- ground pepper
- 2.00 package smoked Polish sausage
- 2.00 large onions
- 8.00 clove garlic
- 0.50 c. tomato paste
- 1.00 can reduced-sodium chicken broth
- 1.00 c. dry red wine
- 1.00 tsp. dried thyme
- 4.00 can Great Northern or cannelloni beans

DIRECTIONS

1. In a food processor, pulse bread until large crumbs form (you should have about 6 cups); season with salt and pepper. Set aside.

2. Preheat oven to 375 degrees. In a 6-quart heavy-bottom saucepan, cook sausage, onions, and garlic, stirring occasionally, until onions are translucent and sausage is starting to brown, 15 to 20 minutes.

3. Add tomato paste, broth, wine, thyme, and 2 cups water; bring to a boil. Reduce to a simmer; add beans. Simmer, stirring occasionally, until slightly thickened but still soupy, about 10 minutes.

4. Stir in 2 cups of the breadcrumbs. Divide sausage mixture between two 3-quart shallow baking dishes or eight 10-ounce ramekins. Top with remaining breadcrumbs.

5. Bake, on a baking sheet, until topping is golden, 30 minutes.

25. Pastitsio

TOTAL TIME: 1:30
PREP: 0:50
LEVEL: MODERATE
SERVES: 8

INGREDIENTS
- 1 lb. penne
- 2 lb. ground lamb
- 2 medium onions
- 0.50 c. red wine
- 1 can tomato paste
- 0.50 tsp. ground cinnamon
- **salt**
- **Pepper**
- 6 tbsp. butter
- 0.50 c. all-purpose flour
- 3 c. milk
- 0.13 tsp. cayenne pepper (optional)
- 0.25 c. grated Parmesan cheese

DIRECTIONS

1. Preheat oven to 375 degrees F. Cook pasta, and drain; reserve. Meanwhile, in a large saucepan, over medium heat, cook lamb, breaking apart pieces with a wooden spoon, until no longer pink, 6 to 8 minutes. Add onions; cook, stirring occasionally, until translucent, about 5 minutes.

2. Transfer to a colander; drain fat, and discard. Return lamb to pan; add wine. Cook over medium heat until almost all liquid has evaporated, about 5 minutes.

3. Stir in tomato paste, cinnamon, and 2 cups water; simmer, stirring occasionally, until thickened, 15 to 20 minutes. Season with salt and pepper.

4. Make Parmesan cheese sauce while mixture is simmering: In a medium saucepan, melt butter over medium heat; whisk in flour until incorporated, about 30 seconds. In a slow steady stream, whisk in milk until there are no lumps.

5. Cook, whisking often, until mixture is thick and bubbly and coats the back of a wooden spoon, 6 to 8 minutes. Stir in cayenne, if desired, and Parmesan.

6. Add pasta to lamb mixture; transfer to a 9-by-13-inch baking dish. Pour sauce over the top, smoothing with the back of a spoon until level. Bake until browned in spots, 35 to 40 minutes. Remove from oven; let cool 15 minutes before serving.

26. Pull-Apart Cheesy Onion Bread

TOTAL TIME: 1:10
COOK: 0:30
LEVEL: MODERATE
YIELD: MAKES ONE 9-INCH LOAF

INGREDIENTS
- 1.50 stick cold unsalted butter
- 1 large onion
- 1 tbsp. poppy seeds
- kosher salt
- Freshly ground pepper
- 1 c. coarsely shredded Gruyère cheese
- 2 c. all-purpose flour
- 2 tsp. baking powder
- 0.50 tsp. baking soda
- 1 tsp. salt
- 1 c. buttermilk

DIRECTIONS
1. Preheat the oven to 425 degrees F. Butter a 9- by 4 1/2-inch metal loaf pan. In a large skillet, melt the 1/2 stick of uncubed butter; pour 2 tablespoons of the melted butter into a small bowl, and reserve. Add the chopped onion to the skillet and cook over moderate heat, stirring occasionally, until it is softened, about 8 minutes. Stir in the poppy seeds and season with salt and pepper. Scrape the onion mixture onto a plate and refrigerate for 5 minutes, until cooled slightly. Stir in the Gruyère.
2. Meanwhile, in a food processor, pulse the flour with the baking powder, baking soda, and salt. Add the cubed butter and pulse until it is the size of small peas. Add the buttermilk and pulse 5 or 6 times, just until a soft dough forms.
3. Turn the dough out onto a well-floured work surface and knead 2 or 3 times. Pat or roll the dough into a 2- by 24-inch rectangle. Spread the onion mixture on top. Cut the dough crosswise into 10 pieces. Stack 9 pieces onion side up, then top with the final piece, onion-side down. Carefully lay the stack in the prepared loaf pan and brush with the reserved butter.
4. Bake the loaf in the center of the oven for about 30 minutes, until it is golden and risen. Let the bread cool for at least 15 minutes before unmolding and serving.

27. Crispy French Fries

LEVEL: MODERATE

SERVES: 8

INGREDIENTS

- 6 large russet potatoes (3 1/2 pounds)
- 1.50 qt. vegetable oil
- **salt**
- ketchup

DIRECTIONS

1. Note: To make perfect fries, cook the potatoes twice.
2. Scrub potatoes, but do not peel. Cut them into halves, lengthwise. Then cut each half into 6 wedges (12 slices per potato). Place in a bowl and cover with cold water; let sit 30 minutes.
3. Heat 4 to 5 inches of oil in a deep fryer or a deep, heavy pot with a candy thermometer. Heat oil to 330 degrees F. Drain and dry potatoes thoroughly with paper towels. Have a plate with 3 layers of paper towels ready. In small batches, fry potatoes until oil spattering stops, about 3 minutes. With a slotted spoon, remove and place on prepared plate. Fries will not be crisp or brown yet.
4. Increase heat of oil to 365 to 370 degrees F. Prepare a new plate with paper towels. Repeat the cooking in small batches until potatoes are golden brown and crisp. Remove and keep warm. Salt fries while hot. Serve with ketchup.

28. Hearty Chicken Noodle Soup

LEVEL: MODERATE

SERVES: 10

INGREDIENTS

- 4 qt. homemade or canned chicken broth
- 1 cleaned whole chicken
- 6 large carrots
- 2 medium onions
- 3 stalk celery
- 2 tbsp. minced fresh parsley
- 1 tbsp. minced fresh dill
- 0.50 lb. medium egg noodles
- **salt**
- Freshly ground pepper

DIRECTIONS

1. In a large pot combine broth and chicken. Bring to a boil; reduce heat, cover, and simmer for 40 minutes, or until juices run clear. Remove chicken from pot and set aside until cool enough to handle. Strain broth. (Chicken and broth may be prepared to this point a day ahead and refrigerated.)

2. Return broth to pot and bring to a boil. Add carrots, onions, and celery. Simmer until vegetables are tender, about 20 minutes.

3. Shred meat from chicken, discarding skin and bones. Tear into small pieces. Add chicken meat back into pot along with herbs and noodles. Increase heat to medium-high and continue to cook until noodles are just tender, about 6 to 8 minutes. Season to taste with salt and freshly ground pepper.

29. Zesty Vegetable Lasagna

TOTAL TIME: 2:10
COOK: 1:30
LEVEL: MODERATE
SERVES: 15

INGREDIENTS

- 2.50 c. ricotta cheese
- 1 c. Pecorino Romano cheese
- 3 clove garlic
- 1 tbsp. dried oregano
- 1 tbsp. dried basil
- 1 large egg
- 1 tsp. salt, pepper, crushed red pepper
- 2 tbsp. extra-virgin olive oil
- 1 lb. cremini mushrooms
- 1 large onion
- 2 red and yellow bell peppers
- 12 oz. fresh baby spinach
- 4.50 c. marinara sauce
- 1 lb. no-boil lasagna noodles
- 1.50 lb. fresh mozzarella cheese

DIRECTIONS

1. Make the fillings: Combine the ricotta and Pecorino Romano cheeses, garlic, herbs, and egg with 1/2 teaspoon each of salt and pepper and the crushed red pepper in a bowl and set aside. Heat 1 tablespoon oil in a large skillet over medium-high heat. Add the mushrooms and cook until golden, about 3 minutes. Add the remaining tablespoon of oil, onions, and peppers and cook until slightly softened, about 4 more minutes. Add the spinach and remaining 1/2 teaspoon each of salt and pepper. Toss and cook until spinach is wilted and tender, about 2 minutes. Set aside.

2. Assemble the lasagna: Heat oven to 350 degrees F. Pour 1 1/2 cups sauce into a deep-dish lasagna pan. Layer 5 lasagna noodles over the sauce. Top with half of the cooked vegetables and a third of the mozzarella. Layer with 5 more noodles and spread half the ricotta mixture over the noodles. Top with 1 cup of sauce and add another layer of noodles. Add the remaining vegetables, another third of the mozzarella, and a layer of noodles. Spread on the remaining ricotta mixture, 1 cup of sauce, and the last layer of noodles. Add the remaining sauce and mozzarella. Cover with foil and bake until bubbly, about 1 hour, 20 minutes. Let the lasagna cool slightly before serving.

30. Cheese Grits And Corn Pudding

TOTAL TIME: 1:35
PREP: 0:25
LEVEL: MODERATE
YIELD: 8 PUDDINGS

INGREDIENTS
- 1.50 c. whole milk
- **salt**
- Freshly ground pepper
- 0.25 c. grits
- 0.50 can creamed corn
- 3 oz. aged Cheddar
- 3 large eggs

DIRECTIONS

1. Preheat oven to 375 degrees F. In a small saucepan over medium heat, bring milk to a simmer. Add 1/2 teaspoon salt; then, stirring constantly, add grits in a slow, steady stream. Continue cooking, stirring occasionally, until grits thicken, about 25 minutes. Transfer to a large bowl and set aside to cool slightly.

2. Meanwhile, purée corn in a food processor. Then, stir corn, Cheddar, and 2 egg yolks into grits. Season with 1/2 teaspoon salt and 1/4 teaspoon pepper. In a large bowl and using an electric mixer, beat egg whites until stiff peaks form. Using a rubber spatula, gently fold egg whites, in thirds, into corn mixture. Divide mixture among eight 1-cup ramekins; set on a baking pan. Bake until puddings puff up, 40 to 45 minutes.

31. Pimiento Cheese And Bacon Crostini

TOTAL TIME: 2:30
LEVEL: MODERATE
YIELD: 3 CUPS OR 40 CROSTINI

INGREDIENTS
- 2.50 c. shredded extra-sharp white cheddar cheese
- 2.50 c. shredded extra-sharp orange cheddar cheese
- 1 7-ounce jar pimientos
- 0.75 c. mayonnaise
- 0.50 tsp. Freshly ground black pepper
- 0.50 tsp. garlic powder
- cayenne pepper
- 40 slice baguette
- 4 strip cooked bacon

DIRECTIONS
1. In a mixer fitted with the paddle, combine the white and orange cheddar cheeses. Add the chopped pimientos, mayonnaise, black pepper, and garlic powder; blend at low speed. Season the pimiento cheese with cayenne pepper to taste. Cover and refrigerate for 2 hours.
2. Preheat the oven to 400° Spread the pimiento cheese on the toasts, top with the bacon, and bake until the cheese is melted and browned, about 2 minutes. Serve.

32. Herbed Potato Gratin With Roasted Garlic And Manchego

TOTAL TIME: 3:00
COOK: 2:30
LEVEL: MODERATE
SERVES: 12

INGREDIENTS
- 3 head garlic
- 1 tbsp. extra-virgin olive oil
- 1 qt. half-and-half
- 1 tbsp. chopped thyme
- 1 tsp. chopped rosemary
- Salt and freshly ground pepper
- 5 lb. Yukon gold potatoes
- 9 oz. aged Manchego cheese
- 5 oz. San Simón or smoked Gouda cheese

DIRECTIONS

1. Preheat the oven to 375°F. In a 9-inch cake pan, drizzle the garlic with the oil. Cover with foil and roast for 40 minutes, until tender. Let cool, then squeeze out the cloves.

2. Mash the garlic to a paste and transfer to a saucepan. Add the half-and-half, thyme, and rosemary and bring to a boil. Simmer over very low heat until reduced to 3 cups, 20 minutes; season with salt and pepper.

3. Arrange one-fourth of the potatoes in the bottom of a 9-by-13-inch baking dish. Top with one-fourth of the shredded cheeses and drizzle lightly with the garlic cream. Repeat the layering with the remaining potatoes, cheese, and cream. Pour any remaining cream on top and press the top layer of potatoes to submerge it.

4. Bake the gratin for about 1 1/2 hours, until golden and bubbling. Let cool for 20 minutes before cutting into squares and serving.

33. Mashed Potatoes With Crispy Shallots

TOTAL TIME: 0:45

LEVEL: MODERATE

SERVES: 12

INGREDIENTS

- 6 lb. Yukon gold potatoes
- 4 clove peeled garlic
- 2 c. canola oil
- 6 large shallots
- 1 c. half-and-half
- 12 tbsp. unsalted butter
- kosher salt

DIRECTIONS
1. In a large pot, cover the quartered potatoes and garlic cloves with cold water and bring to a boil. Simmer over moderate heat until the potatoes are tender when pierced with a fork, about 20 minutes.
2. Meanwhile, in a medium skillet, heat the canola oil until shimmering. Add the shallots in a single layer and cook over moderate heat, stirring frequently, until they are golden, about 15 minutes. Using a slotted spoon, transfer the shallots to paper towels to drain.
3. Drain the potatoes and garlic in a colander, shaking out the excess water. Add the half-and-half and butter to the pot and heat until melted. Remove from the heat. Press the potatoes and garlic through a ricer into the pot and season with salt. Stir and cook over moderate heat until very hot. Transfer the mashed potatoes to a bowl. Just before serving, sprinkle the shallots with salt and garnish the potatoes with the shallots.

34. Simple Shepherd's Pie

TOTAL TIME: 0:50
PREP: 0:25
LEVEL: EASY
YIELD: 8 SERVINGS

INGREDIENTS

- 2 tbsp. extra-virgin olive oil
- 3 small carrots
- 1 c. frozen pearl onions
- 1 lb. lean ground turkey
- 1 tbsp. all-purpose flour
- 1 c. frozen peas
- 2.50 tsp. chopped fresh rosemary
- **salt**
- Freshly ground pepper
- 0.75 c. low-sodium chicken broth
- 3 c. leftover mashed potatoes

DIRECTIONS

1. Preheat oven to 400 degrees F. In a large pan, heat olive oil over medium heat. Add carrots and onions and cook until soft, about 5 minutes. Add turkey and cook, breaking up meat with a wooden spoon, until browned, about 6 minutes. Stir in flour and cook 3 more minutes. Stir in peas and rosemary. Season with salt and pepper. Pour in chicken broth and stir. Bring to a simmer and cook until slightly thickened, about 5 minutes. Season with more salt and pepper. Transfer to a 9- to 10-inch deep-dish pie pan.
2. Spread mashed potatoes atop turkey mixture. Bake until golden on top and heated through, about 25 minutes.

35. Traditional Lasagna Bolognese

LEVEL: MODERATE

YIELD: SERVES 10 TO 12

INGREDIENTS
- Bolognese Sauce
- 3.00 lb. fresh ricotta cheese
- 3.00 large egg yolks
- 1.00 c. grated Parmesan cheese
- 1.50 tsp. Coarse salt
- 0.25 tsp. Freshly ground black pepper
- 0.25 tsp. ground nutmeg
- pinch ground cayenne pepper
- 2.00 tbsp. extra-virgin olive oil
- 1 tbsp. Coarse salt
- 1.00 lb. Uncooked lasagna noodles
- 1.00 lb. fresh mozzarella cheese

DIRECTIONS

1. Bring sauce to room temperature. In a large bowl, whisk together ricotta, egg yolks, Parmesan, 1 1/2 teaspoons salt, black pepper, nutmeg, and cayenne pepper. Chill filling until ready to assemble lasagna.

2. Preheat oven to 400 degrees. Butter an 11-by-14-by-3-inch lasagna baking pan. Bring a large pot of water to a boil. Add olive oil and remaining tablespoon of salt. One at a time, add lasagna noodles; cook until very al dente, 2 to 3 minutes less than the manufacturer's instructions. Remove noodles with tongs; drain in a colander.

3. Spread about 3 cups of sauce on the bottom of the prepared baking dish. Place a single layer of lasagna noodles over the sauce, overlapping them slightly. Spread about 2 cups sauce over the noodles and about half the ricotta filling mixture over the sauce.

4. Top with a layer of lasagna noodles, again slightly overlapping them. Repeat with more sauce and remaining ricotta filling mixture. Top with a final layer of lasagna noodles. Spread a layer of sauce over the noodles, and finish with a layer of sliced mozzarella rounds.

5. Bake until the sauce is bubbling and the cheese is melted, at least 1 hour. Cover with aluminum foil if the cheese starts to brown too early. Let the lasagna stand 10 to 15 minutes before serving.

36. Macaroni And Cheese

TOTAL TIME: 1:00
PREP: 0:30
LEVEL: EASY
SERVES: 8

INGREDIENTS
- Coarse salt and ground pepper
- 1.00 lb. elbow pasta
- 4.00 tbsp. butter
- 1.00 small onion
- 0.25 c. all-purpose flour (spooned and leveled)
- 4.00 c. milk
- 0.13 tsp. cayenne pepper (optional)
- 1.25 c. shredded yellow cheddar cheese
- 1.25 c. shredded white cheddar cheese
- 8.00 oz. ham
- 2.00 slice white sandwich bread

DIRECTIONS
1. Preheat oven to 375 degrees. In a large pot of boiling salted water, cook pasta until al dente; drain and reserve. Meanwhile, in a 5-quart heavy pot, melt butter over medium heat. Add onion; cook, stirring occasionally, until softened, 3 to 5 minutes. Whisk in flour to coat onion. In a slow steady stream, whisk in milk until there are no lumps.
2. Cook, whisking often, until mixture is thick and bubbly and coats the back of a wooden spoon, 6 to 8 minutes. Stir in cayenne, if using, and 1 cup each yellow and white cheddar cheese. Season with 1 teaspoon salt and 1/4 teaspoon pepper.
3. Toss pasta with cheese mixture; fold in ham. Transfer to a 9-by-13-inch baking dish or individual dishes. Set aside.

4. In a food processor, pulse bread until large crumbs form. Toss together with remaining 1/4 cup each white and yellow cheddar, and 1/4 teaspoon salt. Top pasta with breadcrumb mixture. Bake until top is golden, about 30 minutes.

5. Note: This recipe makes enough to fill eight 12-to-16-ounce baking dishes. Divide the macaroni and cheese evenly, sprinkle with topping, and bake for 15 to 20 minutes, until golden.

37. Fried Chicken

LEVEL: EASY

INGREDIENTS
- 3.00 tbsp. Coarse salt
- 2- to 3-pound chicken
- 3.00 c. nonfat buttermilk
- 3.00 tbsp. Tabasco (optional)
- 1.50 c. sifted all-purpose flour
- Freshly ground black pepper to taste
- 2.00 lb. vegetable shortening

DIRECTIONS

1. In a medium container, combine ice water and 2 tablespoons salt; add chicken. Be sure water completely covers chicken. Cover, and refrigerate overnight.
2. Place buttermilk in a medium airtight container. Add chicken pieces, turning to coat in liquid. Cover, and refrigerate at least 8 hours and up to overnight.
3. Swirl Tabasco into buttermilk mixture. Transfer chicken to a wire rack to drain.
4. Line a baking sheet with parchment. Set aside. Place flour, remaining 1 tablespoon salt, and pepper in a large, shallow dish. Mix to combine. Lightly coat chicken in flour mixture. Tap to remove excess. Transfer to prepared baking sheet.
5. Heat vegetable shortening in a deep 12-inch pot over medium-high heat to 350 degrees. Use tongs to place chicken pieces in oil. Fry until deep mahogany color is achieved, about 18 minutes, turning every 7 to 8 minutes. An instant-read thermometer inserted into a thigh should register 170 degrees. Transfer to a wire rack to drain. Season with salt.

38. Chili Pot Pie With Polenta Crust

TOTAL TIME: 1:50
LEVEL: MODERATE
SERVES: 10

INGREDIENTS
Chili:

- 2 tsp. olive oil
- 1.50 lb. well-trimmed boneless beef chuck
- **salt**
- 1 medium onion
- 1 medium red pepper
- 3 clove garlic
- 1 serrano or jalapeño chile
- 2 tbsp. tomato paste
- 3 tbsp. chili powder
- 1 tbsp. ground cumin
- 1 can whole tomatoes in juice
- 2 can red kidney beans

Polenta Crust:

- 2 c. low fat (1%) milk
- 1.50 c. cornmeal
- **salt**
- 4.50 c. boiling water

DIRECTIONS
1. To prepare chili: In 12-inch skillet, with broiler-safe handle (if not broiler-safe, wrap handle in double thickness of foil for broiling in oven later), heat oil on medium-high until hot. Sprinkle beef with 1/4 teaspoon salt. Add beef to skillet in 2 batches, and cook 4 to 5 minutes per batch or until beef is

browned on all sides, stirring occasionally and adding more oil if necessary. With slotted spoon, transfer beef to bowl once it is browned.

2. After all beef is browned, add onion, pepper, garlic, and serrano chile to same skillet, and cook on medium 8 minutes or until all vegetables are lightly browned and tender, stirring occasionally. Stir in tomato paste, chili powder, cumin, and 1/2 teaspoon salt; cook 1 minute, stirring constantly.

3. Return beef, and any juices in bowl, to skillet. Add tomatoes with their juice, stirring and breaking up tomatoes with side of spoon; heat to boiling on medium-high. Reduce heat to low; cover and simmer 1 hour and 15 minutes, stirring occasionally. Add beans and cook Chili, uncovered, 15 minutes longer or until meat is tender.

4. After adding beans to Chili, prepare Polenta Crust: In microwave-safe deep 4-quart bowl or casserole, combine milk, cornmeal, and 3/4 teaspoon salt until blended; whisk in boiling water. Cook in microwave on High 12 to 15 minutes. After first 5 minutes of cooking, whisk vigorously until smooth (mixture will be lumpy at first). Stir 2 more times during cooking.

5. While polenta is cooking, preheat broiler.

6. When Chili is done, skim off fat. Spread polenta evenly over Chili in skillet. Place skillet in broiler 6 to 8 inches from source of heat, and broil polenta 3 to 4 minutes or until lightly browned, rotating skillet if necessary for even browning. Let pot pie stand 10 minutes for easier serving. Makes about 9 cups.

39. Moist Devil's Food Cake With Mrs. Milman's Chocolate Frosting

LEVEL: MODERATE
SERVES: 10

INGREDIENTS

- 1.50 c. unsalted butter
- 0.75 c. unsweetened Dutch-process cocoa powder
- 0.50 c. boiling water
- 3.00 c. sifted cake flour (not self-rising)
- 1.00 tsp. baking soda
- 0.50 tsp. salt
- 2.25 c. sugar
- 4.00 large eggs
- 1.00 tbsp. pure vanilla extract
- 1.00 c. whole milk
- Mrs. Milman's Chocolate Frosting

DIRECTIONS

1. Preheat oven to 350 degrees. Butter three 8-inch round cake pans. Line bottoms with parchment; butter parchment. Dust with cocoa powder; tap out excess. Set aside. Sift cocoa powder into a medium bowl; whisk in boiling water. Set aside to cool.

2. Sift together flour, baking soda, and salt into a large bowl; set aside. Put butter into the bowl of an electric mixer fitted with the paddle attachment. Mix on low speed until creamy. Gradually mix in sugar until pale and fluffy, 3 to 4 minutes. Add eggs, a bit at a time, mixing well between each addition; mix until well blended. Mix in vanilla.

3. Whisk milk into reserved cocoa mixture. With mixer on low speed, add flour mixture to butter mixture in 3 batches, alternating with the cocoa mixture.

4. Divide batter evenly among prepared pans; smooth tops with an offset spatula. Bake, rotating pan halfway through, until a cake tester inserted into centers comes out clean, 35 to 45 minutes. Let cool in pans on wire racks 15 minutes. Turn out cakes onto racks; remove parchment and re-invert. Let cool completely.

5. Using a serrated knife, trim tops of cakes to make level. Place four strips of parchment paper around perimeter of a serving plate or lazy Susan. Place the first layer on the cake plate. Spread the top of the first layer with 1 1/2 cups of frosting. Place the second layer on top and repeat process with another 1 1/2 cups of frosting. Place the remaining layer on top of the second layer, bottom side up. Spread entire cake with remaining 3 cups frosting.

40. Peach Crisps

TOTAL TIME: 1:40
COOK: 1:00
LEVEL: MODERATE
SERVES: 12

INGREDIENTS

- 1 c. all-purpose flour
- 0.25 c. granulated sugar
- 0.25 c. light brown sugar
- 2 tbsp. light brown sugar, combined with above brown sugar
- 0.50 c. rolled oats
- 7 tbsp. cold unsalted butter
- 0.25 tsp. salt
- 3 lb. peaches
- 0.25 c. cornstarch
- Ice cream, optional

DIRECTIONS

1. Make the topping: In a food processor, combine the flour, sugars, oats, butter, and salt and process until the mixture resembles coarse meal.
2. Make the filling: Bring a large pot of water to a boil. Add the peaches and blanch for 1 minute to loosen their skins. Transfer the peaches to a large rimmed baking sheet. When cool enough to handle, peel off the skins and cut the peaches into 1/2-inch dice. Transfer the peaches to a large bowl and sprinkle with the cornstarch. Toss well to coat and let stand for a few minutes.
3. Preheat the oven to 325 degrees F. Butter and sugar 12 5-ounce ramekins and arrange them on a large, rimmed baking sheet. Spoon the peaches into the ramekins and sprinkle with the topping.

4. Bake the crisps for about 1 hour, until the filling is bubbling. Remove the ramekins from the oven and increase the temperature to 400 degrees F. Bake the crisps on the upper rack for about 8 minutes, until the topping is browned. Serve warm or at room temperature with ice cream, if desired.

41. Ganache-Stuffed Chocolate-Chip Cookies

TOTAL TIME: 2:00
COOK: 0:12
LEVEL: MODERATE
YIELD: 18 STUFFED COOKIES

INGREDIENTS
- 1 c. walnuts
- 1 c. all-purpose flour
- 2 tbsp. all-purpose flour
- 1 tsp. baking soda
- 0.50 tsp. salt
- 1 stick unsalted butter
- 0.50 c. packed light brown sugar
- 0.25 c. granulated sugar
- 0.50 tsp. pure vanilla extract
- 1 large egg
- 1 c. bittersweet chocolate chips
- 4 oz. bittersweet chocolate
- 5 tbsp. heavy cream
- 2.50 tbsp. light corn syrup
- 2 tbsp. Crème fraîche

DIRECTIONS
1. Make the cookies: Preheat the oven to 375°. Spread the nuts in a pie plate and toast for 8 minutes; let cool, then chop.
2. In a bowl, mix the flour, baking soda, and salt. In the bowl of a standing mixer fitted with the paddle (or using a hand-held mixer), cream the butter with the sugars and vanilla at medium speed, about 1 minute. Beat in the egg. With the mixer at low speed, beat in the dry ingredients. Beat in the walnuts and

chocolate chips. Spoon level tablespoons of the dough onto 2 ungreased baking sheets, about 2 inches apart. Refrigerate for 30 minutes, until firm.

3. Make the ganache: Put the chocolate in a bowl. In a saucepan, bring the cream and corn syrup to a boil; pour over the chocolate and let stand for 1 minute. Whisk until smooth. Whisk in the crème fraîche. Refrigerate the ganache, stirring occasionally, until thick and spreadable, 1 hour.

4. Bake the cookies for 12 minutes, until golden; let cool on the sheets for 2 minutes, then transfer to a rack to cool completely.

5. Sandwich the chocolate-chip cookies with the ganache and serve.

42. Brownie Sundae Cups

TOTAL TIME: 0:50
PREP: 0:20
LEVEL: MODERATE
YIELD: 6 SERVINGS
SERVES: 6

INGREDIENTS
Brownie Cups

- 1 c. all-purpose flour
- 0.50 c. unsweetened cocoa
- 1 tsp. baking powder
- 0.25 tsp. salt
- 0.75 c. butter or margarine
- 1.50 c. sugar
- 3 large eggs
- 2 tsp. vanilla extract

Hot Fudge Sauce

- 0.50 c. sugar
- 0.33 c. unsweetened cocoa
- 0.25 c. heavy or whipping cream
- 2 tbsp. butter or margarine
- 1 tsp. vanilla extract
- 1 pt. vanilla ice cream

DIRECTIONS
1. Preheat oven to 350 degrees F. Grease 6 jumbo muffin-pan cups (about 4 by 2 inches each) or six 6-ounce custard cups.
2. Prepare Brownie Cups: On waxed paper, combine flour, cocoa, baking powder, and salt. In 3-quart saucepan, melt butter

over medium-low heat. Remove saucepan from heat; stir in sugar. Add eggs and vanilla; stir until well mixed. Stir in flour mixture just until blended. Spoon batter evenly into muffin-pan cups.

3. Bake brownies 30 to 35 minutes or until toothpick inserted in center comes out almost clean. Cool in pan on wire rack 5 minutes. Run tip of thin knife around edge of brownies to loosen. Invert brownies onto rack and cool 10 minutes longer to serve warm, or cool completely to serve later.

4. While Brownie Cups cool, prepare Hot Fudge Sauce: In heavy 1-quart saucepan, heat sugar, cocoa, cream, and butter to boiling over medium-high heat, stirring frequently. Remove saucepan from heat; stir in vanilla. Serve sauce warm, or cool completely, then cover and refrigerate for up to 2 weeks. Gently reheat before using. Makes about 2/3 cup.

5. Assemble brownie sundaes: With small knife, cut 1 1/2- to 2-inch circle in center of each brownie; remove top and set aside. Scoop out brownie centers, making sure not to scoop through bottom of brownies. Transfer centers to small bowl and reserve to sprinkle over ice cream another day. Place each Brownie Cup on a dessert plate. Scoop ice cream into brownie cups and drizzle with hot fudge sauce; replace brownie tops.

43. Brownie Coconut Ice Cream Sandwiches

TOTAL TIME: 1:20
PREP: 0:40
LEVEL: MODERATE
YIELD: 36 SANDWICHES

INGREDIENTS

- 12 oz. raspberries
- 1.50 c. sugar
- 2 tbsp. sugar
- 1 c. unsalted butter
- 8 oz. bittersweet chocolate
- 4 large eggs
- 1.50 c. all-purpose flour
- 0.75 c. cream of coconut (not coconut milk)
- 1.50 c. heavy cream

DIRECTIONS

1. Heat oven to 350 degrees F. Line two 9- by 13-inch baking pans with nonstick foil, leaving a 3-inch overhang on two sides. In a large bowl, toss the berries with 2 tablespoons sugar. Let sit, tossing occasionally, for at least 30 minutes.
2. Meanwhile, place the butter and the chocolate in a medium saucepan and cook, stirring, over medium-low heat until melted. Remove from heat and whisk in the remaining 1 1/2 cups sugar, then the eggs. Add the flour and stir until smooth.
3. Divide the batter between the prepared baking pans. Bake until a wooden pick inserted in the center comes out with moist crumbs attached, 12 to 15 minutes. Let cool completely in the pan.
4. Using an electric mixer, beat the cream of coconut and cream in a large bowl until stiff peaks form. Gently fold the berries and

their juices into the coconut-cream mixture; spoon the cream-berry mixture over one pan of brownies.

5. Use the foil overhangs to lift the remaining brownie layer out of the pan. Invert onto a cutting board and gently peel away the foil. Invert again onto a cookie sheet and gently slide on top of the cream-berry mixture. Cover and freeze for at least 6 hours or up to 2 days.

6. Use the foil overhangs to lift and transfer to a cutting board. Let sit for 5 minutes, then cut into bars.

44. S'mores Pizzas

TOTAL TIME: 1:00
PREP: 0:30
LEVEL: EASY
SERVES: 10

INGREDIENTS
- 0.75 c. coarsely crumbled graham crackers
- 2 tbsp. light brown sugar
- 2 tbsp. granulated sugar
- 1 tbsp. unsalted butter
- 0.25 tsp. pure vanilla extract
- 1 pinch salt
- all-purpose flour
- 1 lb. store-bought pizza dough
- vegetable oil
- 2 bars semisweet chocolate
- 1 c. mini marshmallows
- confectioners' sugar

DIRECTIONS

1. Set a pizza stone on the bottom of the oven and set a rack on the top shelf. Preheat the oven to 500 degrees F and heat the stone for at least 45 minutes. In a food processor, combine the crumbled graham crackers with the brown and granulated sugars and the butter, vanilla, and salt. Process the mixture to fine crumbs.

2. On a lightly floured work surface, roll out each piece of pizza dough to a 12-inch round. Transfer 1 round of dough to a lightly floured pizza peel. Very lightly drizzle the round with vegetable oil and gently rub the oil over the dough.

3. Slide the dough onto the hot stone and bake for about 2 minutes, until it starts to brown on the bottom and puff on top. Using 2 large spatulas, remove the pizza crust and sprinkle it with half of the graham cracker crumbs, half of the chocolate, and half of the marshmallows. Return the pizza to the stone and bake for 1 minute. Transfer the pizza to the top shelf of the oven and bake for about 1 minute, until the marshmallows are browned.

4. Sift confectioners' sugar on top. Cut the pizza into wedges and serve right away. Repeat with the remaining dough, oil, graham cracker crumbs, chocolate, and marshmallows to make a second pizza.

45. Avocado Salsa

Ingredients

6 medium roma tomatoes (20 oz), seeded and diced

1 cup chopped red onion, chopped

1 large or 2 small jalapeños, seeded and chopped (1/4 cup. Leave seeds if you like heat)

3 medium avocados, semi-firm but ripe, peeled, cored and diced

3 1/2 Tbsp olive oil

3 Tbsp fresh lime juice

1 clove garlic, finely minced

1/2 tsp salt (more or less to taste as desired)

1/4 tsp freshly ground black pepper

1/2 cup loosely packed cilantro leaves, chopped

Directions

- Place red onion in a strainer or sieve and rinse under cool water to remove harsh bite. Drain well. Add to a mixing bowl along with diced tomatoes, jalapeños and avocados.

● In a separate small mixing bowl whisk together olive oil, lime juice, garlic, salt and pepper until mixture is well blended. Pour mixture over avocado mixture, add cilantro then gently toss mixture to evenly coat. Serve with tortilla chips or over Mexican entrees.

46. Classic Chicken And Dumplings

Yield: Makes 8 servings

Total time: 2 Hours, 25 Minutes

Ingredients
1 (3 3/4-lb.) whole chicken
1/2 teaspoon garlic powder
1/2 teaspoon dried thyme
2 1/2 teaspoons salt, divided
3/4 teaspoon pepper, divided
1 teaspoon chicken bouillon granules
3 cups self-rising flour
1/2 teaspoon poultry seasoning
1/3 cup shortening
2 teaspoons bacon drippings
1 cup milk
Garnish: chopped fresh parsley

Directions

1. Bring chicken, water to cover, garlic powder, thyme, 1 1/2 tsp. salt, and 1/2 tsp. pepper to a boil in a Dutch oven over medium heat. Cover, reduce heat to medium-low, and simmer 1 hour. Remove chicken; reserve broth.
2. Cool chicken 30 minutes; skin, bone, and shred chicken. Skim fat from broth. Add chicken, bouillon, and remaining 1 tsp. salt and 1/4 tsp. pepper to broth. Return to a simmer.
3. Combine flour and poultry seasoning in a bowl. Cut in shortening and bacon drippings with a pastry blender until crumbly. Stir in milk. Turn dough out onto a lightly floured surface. Roll to 1/8-inch thickness; cut into 1-inch pieces.
4. Drop dumplings, a few at a time, into simmering broth, stirring gently. Cover and simmer, stirring often, 25 minutes. Garnish, if desired.
*2 tsp. butter plus 1/4 tsp. salt may be substituted.

47. Classic Potato Latkes

Yield:
6 servings (serving size: 2 latkes and 2 tablespoons applesauce)
Ingredients
3 1/2 cups shredded peeled baking potato (about 1 1/2 pounds)
1 1/4 cups grated onion
6 tablespoons all-purpose flour
1 teaspoon chopped fresh thyme
1/2 teaspoon kosher salt
1/4 teaspoon freshly ground black pepper
1 large egg
1/4 cup olive oil, divided
3/4 cup unsweetened applesauce
Dash of ground cinnamon
Directions
1. Combine potato and onion in a colander. Drain 30 minutes, pressing with the back of a spoon until barely moist. Combine potato mixture, flour, and next 4 ingredients (through egg) in a large bowl; toss well.
2. Heat a large skillet over medium-high heat. Add 2 tablespoons olive oil to pan, and swirl to coat. Spoon 1/4 cup potato mixture loosely into a dry measuring cup. Pour mixture into pan, and flatten slightly. Repeat procedure 5 times to form 6 latkes. Sauté 3 1/2 minutes on each side or until golden brown. Remove latkes from pan, and keep warm. Repeat procedure with the remaining 2 tablespoons olive oil and potato mixture to yield 12 latkes total. Combine applesauce and ground cinnamon in a bowl. Serve applesauce with latkes.

48. Hello Yummy Bars

Ingredients
3/4 cup butter, melted

1 box chocolate chip Teddy Graham cookies, finely crushed

1 bag English Toffee bits (in the baking section)

1 cup semisweet chocolate chips

1 cup chopped pecans or shredded coconut

1 can (14-oz) sweetened condensed milk

Directions
1. Preheat oven to 325°F.

2. Line a 9" x 13" pan with nonstick foil, allowing it to extend over the ends of the pan. Pour the melted butter into the pan. Sprinkle the cookie crumbs in the bottom of the pan and press firmly. Bake for 5 minutes.

3. Layer the toffee bits, chocolate, and pecans or shredded coconut over the crust in the pan, pressing each layer down firmly. Pour the condensed milk on top. Bake for 30 minutes, or until the edges are lightly browned. Cool on the counter and then put the pan in the refrigerator for a couple of hours before trying to remove the dessert from the pan.

4. Lift the foil out of the pan, turn the bars over, and use a serrated knife to cut them into squares.

49. Mom's Pecan Pie

Yield: Makes 8 Servings

Ingredients
1 1/2 cups pecan pieces
3 large eggs
1 cup sugar
3/4 cup light or dark corn syrup
2 tablespoons melted butter
2 teaspoons vanilla extract
1/2 teaspoon salt
1 (9-inch) deep-dish frozen unbaked pie shell

Directions

1. Spread pecans in a single layer on a baking sheet.
2. Bake at 350° for 8 to 10 minutes or until toasted.
3. Stir together eggs and next 5 ingredients; stir in pecans. Pour filling into pie shell.
4. Bake at 350° for 55 minutes or until set, shielding pie with aluminum foil after 20 minutes to prevent excessive browning. Serve warm or cold.

50. Caramel Cake

Yield: Makes 8 Servings

Ingredients
1 (8-oz.) container sour cream
1/4 cup milk
1 cup butter, softened
2 cups sugar
4 large eggs
2 3/4 cups all-purpose flour
2 teaspoons baking powder
1/2 teaspoon salt
1 teaspoon vanilla extract
Caramel Frosting

Directions
1. Preheat oven to 350°. Combine sour cream and milk.
2. Beat butter at medium speed with an electric mixer until creamy. Gradually add sugar, beating well. Add eggs, 1 at a time, beating until blended after each addition.
3. Combine flour, baking powder, and salt; add to butter mixture alternately with sour cream mixture, beginning and ending with flour mixture. Beat at medium-low speed until blended after each addition. Stir in vanilla. Pour batter into 2 greased and floured 9-inch round cake pans.
4. Bake at 350° for 30 to 35 minutes or until a wooden pick inserted in center comes out clean. Cool in pans on wire racks 10 minutes. Remove from pans to wire racks, and let cool 1 hour or until completely cool.
5. Spread Caramel Frosting between layers and on top and sides of cake.

Part 2

Flax Seeds Vanilla Fruit Scoop

Prep Time: 10 minutes*

Servings: 2

INGREDIENTS

1/2 cup raw walnuts

1/2 cup raw almonds

1/4 cup raw pumpkin seeds

1/4 cup raw sunflower seeds

1/4 cup raw flax seeds

1 cup blueberries

1 cup raspberries

Vanilla Cream

1 cup raw cashews

2 tablespoons raw honey (or dried pitted dates)

1/2 teaspoon vanilla

1/8 teaspoon Celtic sea salt

Water

INSTRUCTIONS

1.*Soak cashews and dates (if using) in enough water to cover at least 6 hours, or overnight in refrigerator. Drain and set aside.

2.Addwalnuts, almonds, pumpkin, sunflower and flax seeds to food processor or high-speed blender. Pulse to coarsely chop. Set aside.

3.For Vanilla Cream, add soaked cashews, honey or dates, vanilla and salt to clean food processor or high-speed blender. Process until smooth, about 1 - 2 minutes. Add enough water or nut milk to reach desired consistency.

4.Spoon layer of fruit into serving dish. Top with chopped nuts. Spoon on layer of Vanilla Cream. Add second layer of chopped nuts. Top with layer of fruit.

5.Serve immediately. Or refrigerate 20 minutes and serve chilled.

Spicy Nutritional Morning Diet

Prep Time: 10 minutes*

Servings: 2

INGREDIENTS

2 coconuts (or 1 cup flaked coconut)

6 dried pitted dates

3 tablespoons whole chia seeds

2 tablespoons cocoa powder

1/2 teaspoon vanilla

1/2 teaspoon ground black pepper

Pinch cayenne pepper

Pinch chili powder

Pinch smoked paprika

Water

INSTRUCTIONS

1. *Soak flaked coconut in 2 cups water overnight in refrigerator, if using. Soak dates in enough water to cover at least 4 hours, or overnight in refrigerator. Drain dates.

2. Add soaked coconut and soaking liquid to high-speed blender. Or remove flesh from fresh coconuts and add to high-speed blender with 2 cups water. Process until well blended and fairly smooth, about 1 - 2 minutes.

3. Strain mixture through nut milk bag, cheesecloth or strainer back into blender.

4. Reserve pulp and set aside to dry and dehydrate, then use as coconut flour.

5.Add dates, cocoa, vanilla and spices to blender. Process until smooth, about 1 minute.

6. Pour mixture into serving dish and stir in chia seeds. Set aside to thicken, about 1 minute.

7.Serve immediately. Or refrigerate 20 minutes and serve chilled.

Raw Honey Strawberry Dish

Prep Time: 10 minutes*
Servings: 2
INGREDIENTS
2 coconuts (or 1 cup flaked coconut)
2 - 4 tablespoons raw honey (or dried pitted dates)
1/4 cup tablespoons whole chia seeds
1 cup strawberries (fresh or frozen and thawed, chopped)
1/2 teaspoon vanilla
Water
INSTRUCTIONS
1.*Soak flaked coconut in 2 cups water overnight in refrigerator, if using. Soak dates in enough water to cover at least 4 hours, or overnight in refrigerator, if using. Drain dates.
2. Add soaked coconut and soaking liquid to high-speed blender. Or remove flesh from fresh coconuts and add to high-speed blender with 2 cups water. Process until well blended and fairly smooth, about 1 - 2 minutes.
3. Strain mixture through nut milk bag, cheesecloth or strainer back into blender.
4. Reserve pulp and set aside to dry and dehydrate, then use as coconut flour.
5. Remove stems from strawberries, then cut in half. Add to blender with honey or dates, and vanilla. Process until smooth, about 1 minute.
6. Pour mixture into serving dish and stir in chia seeds. Set aside to thicken, about 1 minute.

7.Serve immediately. Or refrigerate 20 minutes and serve chilled.

Raw Nuts Banana Bowl

Prep Time: 10 minutes
Servings: 2
INGREDIENTS
1 coconut (1/2 cup flaked coconut)
3/4 cup raw nuts (any combination of cashews, almonds, brazil nuts, acorns, macadamia nuts, etc.)
2 overripe bananas
2 teaspoons ground cinnamon
1/4 teaspoon vanilla
1/4 teaspoon Celtic sea salt
Water
INSTRUCTIONS
1.* Soak nuts in enough water to cover for at least 6 hours, or overnight in refrigerator. Drain and rinse, then set aside. Soak flaked coconut in 2 cups water in refrigerator overnight, if using.
2. Add soaked coconut and soaking liquid to high-speed blender. Or remove flesh from fresh coconut and add to high-speed blender with 2 cups water. Process until well blended and fairly smooth, about 1 - 2 minutes.
3. Strain mixture through nut milk bag, cheesecloth or strainer back into blender or food processor.
4. Reserve pulp and set aside to dry and dehydrate, then use as coconut flour.
5. Peel bananas and add to processor with vanilla, salt and 1 teaspoon cinnamon. Process until thick and mostly smooth, about 1 minute.

6.Transfer to serving dish and serve immediately.

Carrot Orange Salad

Prep Time: 5 minutes
Servings: 1
INSTRUCTIONS

2 large carrots

3 tablespoon dried cranberries

1/4 cup raw almonds

1/2 small orange (or tangerine)

1/2 piece fresh ginger

1/2 teaspoon ground ginger

DIRECTIONS

1.Add carrots to food processor with shredding attachment and process, or grate with grater. Add to medium mixing bowl with cranberries and ground ginger.

2.Add almonds to food processor and pulse to coarsely chop. Or add to paper or plastic kitchen bag and pound with heavy rolling pin to crush. Peel ginger and dice or finely grate. Zest then juice orange. Add to carrot mixture and toss to combine.

3.Transfer to serving dish and serve immediately. Or refrigerate 20 minutes and serve chilled.

Blueberry Pomegranate Salad

Prep Time: 5 minutes

Servings: 1

INSTRUCTIONS

1 apple

1 small banana

1/4 cup blueberries

1/4 cup raw almonds

2 dried pitted dates

2 tablespoons pomegranate seeds (or dried goji or noni berries)

1/4 teaspoon ground cinnamon

INGREDIENTS

1. Core and dice apple. Peel and dice banana. Add to serving dish and mix to combine. Top with blueberries.

2. Chop almonds and dates. Or add to food processor and pulse to coarsely grind.

3. Top fruit with chopped nuts and dates. Sprinkle with pomegranate seeds and cinnamon and serve immediately.

Shred Diet Berries Blend

Prep Time: 10 minutes
Servings: 1
INSTRUCTIONS
1 nectarine
1/2 cup strawberries
1/4 cup blackberries
1/4 cup blueberry
1/4 cup cherries
1/4 cup raw nuts (cashews, almonds, brazil nuts, acorns, macadamia, etc.)
1/2 inch piece fresh ginger
Small sprig fresh mint
INGREDIENTS
1. Cut nectarine in half and remove pit. Dice and add to small mixing bowl. Remove stems from strawberries and quarter. Pit cherries. Add to bowl with blackberries and blueberries.
2. Peel ginger and mince or finely grate. Chiffon mint leaves. Add to bowl and toss to combine. Transfer to serving dish.
3. Add nuts to food processor and pulse to coarsely chop. Or add to paper or plastic kitchen bag and pound with heavy rolling pin to crush.
4. Sprinkle on nuts and serve immediately. Or refrigerate 20 minutes and serve chilled.

Grapefruit Citrus Cream

Prep Time: 10 minutes
Servings: 1
INSTRUCTIONS
1 fresh coconut (or 1/2 cup flaked coconut)
1/4 - 1/3 cup dried pitted dates (or raw honey)
1 blood orange
1 tangerine (or navel orange or clementine)
1/2 grapefruit (ruby red, pink or white)
1/2 lime
1 tablespoon sunflower seeds (optional)
Water
INGREDIENTS
1.*Soak flaked coconut in 1 cup water overnight in refrigerator, if using. Soak dates in enough water to cover overnight in refrigerator. Drain.
2.Add soaked coconut and soaking liquid to high-speed blender. Or remove flesh from fresh coconut and add to high-speed blender with 3/4 cup water. Process until thick and fairly smooth, about 1 - 2 minutes.
3.Strain mixture through nut milk bag, cheesecloth or strainer back into blender or to food processor.
4.Reserve pulp and set aside to dry and dehydrate, then use as coconut flour.
5.Add soaked dates or honey to processor and process until smooth. Set aside.

6.Peel all citrus and cut into segments. Add to serving dish. Top with sweet coconut cream. Sprinkle on sunflower seeds (optional).

7.Serve immediately. Or refrigerate 20 minutes and serve chilled.

Peach Cinnamon Plate

Prep Time: 5 minutes

Servings: 1

INGREDIENTS

2 ripe peaches (or nectarines)

4 dried pitted dates

1/3 cup raw almonds

1/4 teaspoon ground cinnamon

1/4 teaspoon ground ginger

1/8 teaspoon vanilla

1/8 teaspoon ground white pepper (or ground black pepper)

INSTRUCTIONS

1. Add dates, almonds vanilla and spices to food processor or high-speed blender. Pulse to coarsely grind, about 1 minute.

2. Cut peaches in half and remove pits. Dice peaches and transfer to serving dish.

3. Sprinkle on almond mixture and serve immediately.

Blueberry Vanilla Serve

Prep Time: 5 minutes*

Servings: 1

INGREDIENTS

1 1/2 cups raw cashews

1 banana

1/4 cup blueberries

1 tablespoon raw honey (or 2 pitted dates)

1 tablespoon lemon juice

1/4 teaspoon vanilla

1/4 teaspoon Celtic sea salt

Water

INSTRUCTIONS

1.*Soak cashews and dates (if using) in enough water to cover overnight in refrigerator. Drain.

2.Peel banana. Add to food processor or high-speed blender with soaked cashews, dates or honey, lemon juice, vanilla and salt. Process until thick and fairly smooth, about 1 - 2 minutes. Add enough water to reach desired consistency.

3.Transfer to serving dish and top with blueberries. Serve immediately.

Almond Walnuts Morning Fillers

Prep Time: 10 minutes*
Servings: 1
INGREDIENTS
3/4 cup raw almonds
1/3 cups raw walnuts
1/3 cups cashews
1/4 cup raw pumpkin seeds
1/4 cup shredded or flaked coconut
2 tablespoon dried cranberries
1/3 cup dried pitted dates
1/4 tablespoon vanilla
1/4 tablespoon cinnamon
1/4 teaspoon ground ginger
1/2 teaspoon Celtic sea salt
Water
INSTRUCTIONS
1.*Separately oak 1/4 cup almonds in enough water to cover at least 6 hours, or overnight. Drain and rinse. Soak 1/4 cupdates in enough water to cover at least 6 hours, or overnight. Drain.
2.Add soaked almonds to high-speed blender with2/3 - 3/4 cup water. Process until well blended and almost smooth, about 1- 2 minutes.
3.Strain mixture through nut milk bag, cheesecloth or strainer back into blender.

4.Add soaked dates to blender with vanilla, salt and ginger. Process until smooth, about 1 minutes. Add to medium mixing bowl.

5.Chop remaining almonds, walnuts and dates by hand. Or add to clean food processor or high-speed blender and pulse to roughly chop. Add to bowl with pumpkin seeds, flaked coconut, cranberries and cinnamon. Mix to combine.

6.Transfer to serving dish and serve immediately. Or refrigerate 20 minutes and serve chilled.

Apple Walnuts Flax Dish

Prep Time: 5 minutes*

Servings: 2

INGREDIENTS

2 cage free eggs (optional)

1/2 apple

1/4 cup flaked or shredded coconut

1/4 - 1/3 cup dried pitted dates

1/3 cup raw walnuts

1/3 cup raw almonds

2 tablespoons coconut oil (or coconut butter or cacao butter)

2 tablespoons flax seed (or chia seed)

2 tablespoons raisins

2 tablespoons dried goji berries (optional)

1 teaspoon ground cinnamon

Pinch Celtic sea salt

Water

INSTRUCTIONS

1.*Soak walnuts and almonds in enough water to cover for at least 6 hours, or overnight in refrigerator. Drain and rinse, then set aside. Soak dates in enough water to cover for at least 6 hours, or overnight in refrigerator. Drain and set aside.Soak flaked coconut in 1 cup water overnight in refrigerator.

2.Add flax or chia to food processor or high-speed blender and process until finely ground. Add coconut oil and process until thick paste forms.

3.Add dates, nuts, eggs, cinnamon, salt, soaked coconut and soaking liquid to processor. Process until thick mixture forms, about 1 - 2 minutes. Transfer to serving dish.

4.Core and dice apple. Top with dices apple, raisins and goji berries (optional).

5.Serve immediately.

Flax Seed Cinnamon Cakes With Berry Jam

Prep Time: 15 minutes*

Dehydrating Time: 8 - 9 hours

Servings: 2

INGREDIENTS

Pancakes

1 young coconut (plus coconut water)

1/2 cup raw cashews (or 1/4 cup raw cashew butter)

1/4 cup flax seed

1/4 teaspoon ground cinnamon

1/2 teaspoon vanilla

Water

Berry Jam

1 orange

1/4 cup dried raspberries

1/4 cup dried cherries

1/4 cup dried strawberries

Water

INSTRUCTIONS

1.*Soak dried fruit in enough water to cover at least 4 hours, or overnight in refrigerator. Drain and reserve soaking liquid. Set aside.

2.For Pancakes, add flax to food processor or high-speed blender. Process until finely ground, about 2 minutes.

3.Add cashews to processor, if using. Process until smooth, up to 5 minutes. Or use prepared cashew butter.

4.Remove flesh and water from young coconut addand add to processor with cashew butter, cinnamon and vanilla cardamom. Process until smooth batter forms, about 1 - 2 minutes. Add enough water to reach desired consistency.

5.Place parchment paper or dehydrator sheets on dehydrator trays.

6.Use spoon to spread batter on prepared sheets in 2 x 2 inch circles 1/4 inch thick. Place trays in dehydrator and set to 110 degrees F for 6 hours.

7.Remove trays from dehydrator. Flip Pancakes and place trays back in dehydrator. Continue dehydrating 2 - 3 hours, until surface is dry but Pancakes are still moist and pliable.

8.For Berry Jam, zest then juice orange into clean food processor or high-speed blender. Add soaked fruit and process until mostly smooth, about 1 minute. Add enough soaking liquid and/or water to reach desired consistency and sweetness.

9.Remove Pancakes from dehydrator and transfer to serving dish. Top with Berry Jam and serve immediately.

Sugar Free Flax Cake With Apricot Jam

Prep Time: 10 minutes*

Servings: 2

INGREDIENTS

Coconut Breakfast Cake

1 fresh coconut (or 1/2 cup flaked or shredded coconut)

1/2 cup ground flax seed (or chia seed)

1/4 cup raw honey (or 1/3 cup dried pitted dates)

2 tablespoons coconut oil (or coconut butter or cacao butter)

1/2 teaspoon ground cinnamon

1/4 teaspoon Celtic sea salt

Water

Apricot Jam

1 cup dried apricots

2 tablespoons lemon juice

1/4 inch piece fresh ginger (or 1/2 teaspoon ground ginger)

Water

INSTRUCTIONS

1.*For Coconut Breakfast Cakes, soak flaked coconut and in 1 cup water overnight in refrigerator, if using. Soak dates in enough water to cover overnight in refrigerator, if using. Drain.

2.Add soaked coconut and soaking liquid to high-speed blender. Or remove flesh from fresh coconut and add to high-speed blender with 1 cup water, ground flax or chia, soaked dates or honey, coconut oil, salt and cinnamon. Pulse to coarsely grind, until mixture sticks together.

3.Form mixture into 6 balls and flatten into cakes. Or mold in lined muffin tins. Set aside.

4.For Apricot Jam, peel ginger and add to clean food processor or high-speed blender with apricots and lemon juice. Process until smooth, about 1 minute. Add enough water to reach desired consistency.

5.Transfer Coconut Breakfast Cakes to serving dish. Top with Apricot Jam and serve immediately. Or refrigerate 20 minutes and serve chilled.

Nuts & Seeds Toast

Prep Time: 5 minutes

Cook Time: 20 minutes

Servings: 4

INGREDIENTS

1 cup almond flour

1/4 cup ground chia seed (or flax seed meal)

1 tablespoon vanilla

1 teaspoon ground nutmeg

1 teaspoon ground cinnamon

1/2 cup raw agave nectar (or 1/2 cup raw honey + 1 tablespoon water)

1 cup flaked coconut

1 cup sliced almonds

1/2 cup dried figs

1/2 cup dried dates

1/2 cup pecans

1/2 cup pumpkin seeds

1/2 cup dried apricots

1/2 cup coconut oil, melted

INSTRUCTIONS

1. Preheat oven to 350 degrees F. Lightly coat cookie sheet with coconut oil.

2. Stem figs and pit dates. Chop figs, dates, pecans and apricots. Add to medium bowl, along with all other ingredients. Mix to combine then spread evenly over sheet pan with spatula.

3.Bake in preheated oven for about 10 minutes.Then carefully remove and use spatula to turn over par-baked granola.Bake for additional8 -10 minutes.Check periodically to ensure nuts do not over-toast.

4.Remove from oven and let cool and firm. Serve cool.

Almond Meal Vanilla Pancakes

Prep Time: 5 minutes

Cook Time: 15 minutes

Servings: 2

INGREDIENTS

1 3/4 cups almond meal

2 eggs

3/4 cup almond milk

2 medium carrots

1/4 cup chopped walnuts

1/4 cup golden raisins (optional)

1 teaspoon baking powder

1 tablespoon ground cinnamon

1 teaspoon ground nutmeg

1 teaspoon ground ginger

1 teaspoon vanilla

1/4 teaspoon sea salt

Pinch of ground black pepper

INSTRUCTIONS

1. Heat large skillet on medium-high heat and lightly coat with oil.

2. Finely grate carrots and drain in paper towel, or roughly process in food processor or bullet blender.

3. In medium bowl whisk eggs, almond milk, vanilla, cinnamon, nutmeg, ginger and black pepper.

4. Add almond flour, salt and baking powder. Whisk until smooth. Stir in carrots, walnuts and raisins (optional).

5.Use ladle or dry measure cup to pour 1/3 cup of batter onto hot oiled skillet. Fit 2 or 3 pancakes comfortably, so they do not touch as they spread.

6.Cook until sides of pancakes are firm and batter bubbles up a bit. About 3 - 4 minutes.

7.Carefully flip pancakes with spatula and cook for additional minute, or until cooked through. Repeat with remaining batter. Re-oil pan if necessary. Pancakes will be slightly delicate, so flip and plate with care.

8.Serve warm. Sprinkle with cinnamon and drizzle with agave nectar, or topping of choice.

Ground Flax Seed Breakfast Burrito

Prep Time: 10 minutes
Cook Time: 10 minutes
Servings: 2
INGREDIENTS
Tortillas:
2 tablespoons coconut flour
2 tablespoons almond flour
2 teaspoons ground flax seed
2 eggs
2 tablespoons melted coconut oil
1/4 teaspoon baking powder
1/4 - 1/2 cup water
Coconut oil (for cooking)
Filling:
6 oz natural pre-cooked ham
6 eggs
1 bell pepper
1/2 red onion
1 avocado
4 oz organic salsa
Pinch sea salt
Pinch ground black pepper
INSTRUCTIONS

1. Heat largepan over medium-high heat and coat with 2 tablespoons of coconut oil. Heat second skillet over medium heat and lightly coat with coconut oil.
2. For **Tortillas**, blend coconut flour, almond flour, flax meal and baking powder in medium bowl. In separate bowl, whisk together 2 eggs, 2 tablespoons coconut oil and 1/4 cup water.
3. Slowly whisk dry blend into wet mixture. Whisk as you pour to avoid clumps. Continue to whisk and slowly add just enough water to make thin but hearty batter.
4. Once coconut oil is hot, use ladle or dry measure cup to pour half of batter into large pan. Tilt pan in circular motion as you pour so batter spreads thinly. Cook batter for about 2 minutes or until tortilla is slightly golden and firm.
5. While **Tortillas** cook, seed and stem pepper and peel onion. Chop ham, pepper and onion. Add to second skillet and sauté for about 2 minutes.
6. Flip tortilla and cook for 2 more minutes. Remove when toasted and cooked through. Place on paper towel or parchment. Add remaining batter to large pan, repeating tilting process to create thin tortilla.
7. While second tortilla cooks , beat 6 eggs in medium bowl and pour over veggies and ham. Salt and pepper to taste. Scramble until desired firmness.
8. Fill both tortillas down center each with half of ham scramble. Slice avocado in half, pit,then scoop out flesh onto each burrito.
9. Roll up tortillas and plate fold-side down. Dollop with your favorite salsa. Serve warm.

Coconut Flour Breakfast Pizza

Prep Time: 10 minutes
Cook Time: 15 minutes
Servings: 2
INGREDIENTS
Crust:
1 1/2 cup almond flour
1/4 cup tablespoons coconut flour
2 eggs
1 tablespoon melted coconut oil
Coconut oil (for cooking)
Topping:
4 eggs
4 oz pre-cooked natural sausage
1/2 small red onions
1 /2 green pepper
1 whole roasted red pepper (jarred)
Handful black olives
1 tablespoon rosemary
Pinch ground black pepper
Pinch sea salt
INSTRUCTIONS
1. Preheat oven to 425 degrees F. Heat medium skillet to medium heat and lightly coat with coconut oil. Coat 8 or 9-inch round cake pan with coconut oil and dust with coconut flour.
2. Combine all **Crust** ingredients in small bowl. If too soft, add 1 tablespoon of coconut flour at a time. If too firm, add 1

tablespoon of water at a time. Adjust until firm dough that can hold its shape forms.

3.Form dough into ball and place in cake pan. Gently pat it into 1/4 inch thick circle, building up around edge about 1/2 - 1 inch up sides of pan. Bake crust for 5 minutes.

4.Chop sausage and rosemary.Seed and stem green pepper and peel onion. Slice onion and pepper and add to skillet with sausage. Sauté about 2 minutes.

5.Whisk eggs in medium bowl and add eggs to skillet, plus rosemary. Remove skillet from heat and scramble very lightly.

6.Reduce oven to 350 degrees F and remove pan.Carefully pour runny scrambled eggs into crust. Slice roasted red pepper and olivesand sprinkle over eggs. Salt and pepper to taste.

7.Return pizza to oven and bake another 10 - 15 minutes or until eggs firm.

8.Slice and serve hot from pan. Or remove, slice and serve.

Low Carb Romaine Lettuce Salad

Prep Time: 10 minutes
Cook Time: 5 minutes
Servings: 1
INGREDIENTS
Salad:
4 slices turkey bacon
1 tablespoon coconut oil
1 heart of romaine lettuce
2 medium tomatoes, chopped
Dressing:
1 avocado
1/2 small white onion
1 small garlic clove
Juice of 1 lemon
Small bunch of parsley leaves
Pinch sea salt
Pinch ground black pepper
INSTRUCTIONS
1. Heat medium skillet to medium-high heat and add coconut oil.
2. Chop turkey bacon and add to skillet. Browned for 2 - 3 minutes on each side, until thoroughly cooked. Remove turkey bacon and preserve any leftover oil.
3. Rinse and dry heart of romaine, then chop. Dice tomato and toss with lettuce in large bowl.
4. For **Dressing**, slice avocado in half, pit, and spoon flesh into food processor or bullet blender. Add peeled onion and garlic,

lemon juice and parsley.Add excess coconut oil from pan.Process until smooth. Salt and pepper to taste.

5.Use tongs to transfer lettuce and tomatoes to plate. Sprinkle on turkey bacon, and drizzle with avocado **Dressing**. Serve immediately.

Chia Seed Dates Oatmeal

Prep Time: 5 minutes
Cook Time: 10 minutes
Servings: 2
INGREDIENTS
2 cups coconut milk
1/2 cup quick tapioca
1/4 cup chia seed
1/2 cup dried dates
1 small banana
2 tablespoons slivered almonds
2 tablespoons pumpkin seeds
2 tablespoons flaked coconut
2 tablespoons walnuts
1 tablespoon vanilla
1 teaspoon ground cinnamon
2 tablespoons raw agave nectar (optional)
Pinch sea salt
Water
INSTRUCTIONS
1. Heat medium pan over medium heat .
2. Add almonds, pumpkin seeds, coconut flakes and walnuts to hot dry pan. Dry toast about 2 minutes, stirring frequently to prevent burning.
3. Pit and chop dates. Cut banana in half and blend with coconut milk and dates in food processor or bullet blender. Reserve other half of banana.

4.Add milk mixture to hot pan. Add quick tapioca, chia seeds, vanillaand pinch of salt. Stir and thicken over heat about 5 - 8 minutes, or until tapioca is soft. Add water to loosen for runnier "oatmeal."

5.Slice reserved half of banana. Serve hot in bowl. Top with banana slices, sprinkle with cinnamon, and drizzle with agave (optional).

Spicy Almond Meal

Prep Time: 5 minutes
Cook Time: 15 minutes
Servings: 2
INGREDIENTS
Pancakes:
1 3/4 cups almond meal
3/4 cup almond milk
2 eggs
1 teaspoon baking powder
1 teaspoon vanilla
Pinch sea salt
Pinch ground black pepper
Agave nectar (optional)
Coconut oil (for cooking)
Filling:
4 eggs
INSTRUCTIONS
1. Heat large skillet with lid over medium heat and lightly coat with coconut oil.
2. Whisk together 2 eggs, almond milk and vanilla in medium bowl. Whisk in almond flour, baking powder and salt until smooth.
3. Use ladle or dry measure cup to pour 1/3 of batter onto hot oiled skillet in a circle with a hole large enough for one egg. Fit up to 2 pancakes comfortably, so they do not touch as they spread.

4.Crack one egg into each space within pancake. Cover with lid and cook until sides of pancakes are firm and batter bubbles up a bit. About 3 - 4 minutes.

5.Remove lid and gently flip pancakes with spatula, careful to keep yolks intact. Cookuncovered for about 3 minutes, or until pancakesarecooked through.

6.Repeat with remaining batter. Re-oil pan if necessary. Pancakes will be slightly delicate, so flip and plate with care.

7.Sprinkle egg with salt and pepper to taste. Drizzle with agave nectar (optional). Serve warm.

Spicy Bacon With Egg Scramble

Prep Time: 10 minutes
Cook Time: 15 minutes
Servings: 2

INGREDIENTS

6 eggs
4 slices nitrate-free bacon
2 dried figs
1 sweet apple
1 bell pepper
1 small sweet onion
1/2 teaspoon ground black pepper
1/2 teaspoon paprika
1/2teaspoon sea salt
1/2 teaspoon cinnamon (optional)

INSTRUCTIONS

1. Bring small pot to boil with lightly salted water. Heat medium skillet over medium-high heat.
2. Dice bacon and add to hot skillet. Brown bacon for about 3 minutes, stirring occasionally with wooden spatula.
3. Add figs to boiling water for 5 minutes.
4. Peel and core apple. Stem and seed pepper. Peel onion. Dice apple, pepper and onion and add to skillet. Sauté another 2 minutes, until veggies caramelize and bacon crisps.
5. Remove figs from boiling water and dice. Add to skillet, plus spices. Sauté another minute.

6.Crack eggs directly into skillet and scramble gently with wooden spatula.

7.Cook eggs to desired firmness and serve hot.

Egg With Pork Sausage Breakfast Skillet

Prep Time: 5 minutes

Cook Time: 15 minutes

Servings: 2

INGREDIENTS

6 eggs

8 oz ground pork sausage

1 medium sweet potato

1 bell pepper

1 small red onion

Ground black pepper, to taste

Paprika, to taste

sea salt, to taste

Pinch of cinnamon (optional)

INSTRUCTIONS

1. Bring medium pot to boil with lightly salted water. Leave enough room in pot for sweet potato. Heat large skillet over medium-high heat.

2. Peel and dice sweet potato. Add to boiling water for 5 minutes.

3. Add sausage to hot skillet. Brown sausage for 5 minutes, stirring occasionally with wooden spatula.

4. While potatoes and sausage cook, seed and vein bell pepper and peel onion, then dice.

5. Beat eggs with spices in medium bowl with hand mixer or whisk.

6.Once browned, add pepper and onion to sausage. Sauté about 2 minutes, until vegetables are tender and a bit caramelized.

7.Drain sweet potatoes in colander and add to skillet. Sauté about 1 minute, until any excess liquid is evaporated. Then pour in egg mixture.

8.Scramble eggs with wooden spatula. Reduce skillet to medium heat to cook eggs evenly and avoid browning.

9.Cook and stir eggs until desired firmness. Remove from heat and serve.

Almond Meal Banana Pancakes

Prep Time: 5 minutes
Cook Time: 15 minutes
Servings: 2
INGREDIENTS
Pancakes:
1 3/4 cups almond meal
1 teaspoon baking powder
2 eggs
3/4 cup coconut milk
1/4 cup flaked coconut
1/2 banana
1 teaspoon vanilla
1/4 teaspoon sea salt
Coconut oil (for cooking)
Topping:
1/2 banana
Agave nectar (optional)
INSTRUCTIONS
1.Heat a large skillet over medium-high heat and lightly coat with coconut oil.
2.Mash 1/2 banana in medium bowl with fork. Whisk in eggs, then coconut milk and vanilla.
3.Add almond flour, salt and baking powder. Whisk until smooth. Fold in coconut flakes.

4.Use ladle or dry measure cup to pour 1/4 cup of batter onto hot oiled skillet. Fit 2 or 3 pancakes comfortably, so they do not touch as they spread.

5.Cook until sides of pancakes are firm and batter bubbles up a bit. About 3 to 4 minutes.

6.Carefully flip pancakes with spatula and cook for additional minute, or until cooked through. Repeat with remaining batter. Re-oil pan if necessary. Pancakes will be slightly delicate, so flip and plate with care.

7.Slice 1/2 banana. Top with banana slices and agave nectar. Serve warm.

Cinnamon & Pumpkin With Bacon Treat

Prep Time: 5 minutes

Cook Time: 15 minutes

Servings: 2

INGREDIENTS

1 3/4 cups almond flour

1 cup almond milk

1/2 cup pumpkin puree

2 eggs

1 teaspoon baking powder

2 teaspoons ground cinnamon

1 teaspoon vanilla

1/4 teaspoon sea salt

4 slices nitrate-free bacon

INSTRUCTIONS

1.Heat large skillet over high heat.

2.Chop bacon into 1/2 inch pieces. Add to hot skillet and brown. Stir occasionally with wooden spoon.

3.Whisk eggs in medium bowl. Then whisk in almond milk, pumpkin puree, vanilla and cinnamon.

4.Add almond flour, salt and baking powder. Whisk until smooth.

5.Once crisp, reduce pan to medium heat and remove bacon from pan, leaving drippings. Drain bacon bits on paper towel, then stir into pancake mixture.

6.Use ladle or dry measure cup to pour 1/4 cup of batter onto hot oiled skillet. Fit 2 or 3 pancakes comfortably, so they do not touch as they spread.

7.Cook until sides of pancakes are firm and batter bubbles up a bit. About 3 to 4 minutes.

8.Carefully flip pancakes with spatula and cook for additional minute, or until cooked through. Repeat with remaining batter. Pancakes will be slightly delicate, so flip and plate with care.

Serve warm. Top with topping of choice.

Salads

Broccoli Salad

16 ounce bag of broccoli
2 carrots diced
A handful of cranberries (you can use craisins if you don't have fresh)
A handful of cashews
DRESSING:
½ tsp. of salt
½ cup of sugar
½ cup of mayo
¼ cup of vinegar

Mix salad ingredients in a bowl. The combine all dressing ingredients in a small bowl, dress the salad, and enjoy!

Morrocan Carrot Salad

3 large carrots cooked
2 fresh cloves of garlic diced
1 Tbsp. of olive oil
2 Tbsp. of fresh squeezed lemon juice
Salt and pepper to taste

Mix carrots and garlic together in a bowl. Combine olive oil, lemon juice together, add salt and pepper to taste. Pour dressing over carrots and garlic.

Cucumber Salad

3 cucumbers, sliced thin
DRESSING:
3 Tbsp. of mayo
¼ cup of vinegar
1 tsp. of salt
¼ cup of diced onions
½ cup of sugar
Mix dressing ingredients together, combine with the sliced cucumbers.

Chicken Salad

4 cups cooked diced chicken

1 stalk of celery, diced

4 scallions or ¼ of an onion, diced

1 ½ tsp. of fresh tarragon or dill (can use dry)

2 Tbsp. finely chopped parsley (can use dry)

DRESSING:

1 cup of mayo

2 tsp. of fresh lemon juice

1 tsp. of Dijon mustard

2 tsp. of kosher salt

Black pepper to taste

Mix first 5 ingredients together, set aside. Wisk together dressing ingredients, combine dressing and chicken mixture together.

Potatoe Kugel

5 large potatoes (you can use Idaho or Yukon gold)
1 medium onion
1 ½ tsp. of kosher salt
¼ tsp. of freshly ground pepper
2 eggs
¼ cup of canola oil

Peel the potatoes, and cut into quarters.Cut peeled onion into quarters as well.You can hand grate or food process the onions (to a medium shred), then hand grate or food process the potatoes, in a bowl together.Hand drain the liquid from the potatoes and onions.Lightly beat eggs in a separate small bowl, add the salt and the pepper to the eggs.Heat the oil in small saucepan for 3 minutes.Mix the potatoe/onion mixture with the eggs and oil, pour into a 9x13 pan, bake uncovered at 350° for 1 ½ hours.

Sweet Noodle Kugel

8 ounces of medium sized egg noodles

¼ of margarine

4 eggs, beaten

½ cup of sugar

1 Tbsp. of cinnamon

1 Tbsp. of salt

Preheat oven to 350°. Cook noodles in salted water for ten minutes, drain noodles and put into a large bowl. Melt the margarine inside with the hot noodles. After the margarine is melted, add the eggs, sugar, cinnamon and salt and mix well. Pour into greased 8x8 baking dish. Bake for 50 minutes uncovered.

Zucchini Squash Kugel

2 Tbsp. vegetable oil

6 medium zucchinis, peeled and shredded

2 medium onions, diced

6 large eggs

1 1/3 cups all purpose flour

1 cup water

1/3 cup mayo.

¼ cup sugar

2 tsp. of baking powder

2 tsp. of salt

Ground black pepper to taste

In a large skillet heat vegetable oil over medium heat. Sauté zucchinis and onions together for about 10 minutes until soft and transparent. Remove skillet from heat.

Preheat oven to 350°. Mix eggs, flour, water, mayo, sugar, baking powder, salt and black pepper together in a large bowl, add zucchini and onions.

Pour the mixture into a 9x13 pan, bake 1 hour, uncovered until top is crisp and brown.

Apple Cranberry Kugel

4 cups of flour

2 cups of sugar

1 scoop of vanilla sugar

1 scoop baking powder

1 cup oil

2 eggs

5 apples, peeled and sliced thinly

1 can jelled cranberries

Mix first 6 ingredients together in a bowl. Put half of the mixture on the bottom of a 9x13 pan, place sliced apples and cranberries on top. Then spread remaining "crumb" mixture on top. Sprinkle top of kugel with water and sugar, then bake on 350° uncovered for 1 ½ hours.

Chicken

Schnitzel

3 eggs, beaten
6 thin sliced, boneless chicken breasts
2 cups bread crumbs
1 cup corn flake crumbs
Garlic powder, smoked paprika, salt, pepper to taste
¼ of oil for frying
Place eggs in shallow bowl or container. Mix the bread crumbs and corn flakes together in a shallow bowl or container, mix in spices to taste. Add oil to large frying pan and heat pan on medium high heat until oil is gently bubbling. Take chicken cutlet and dip in bread crumbs first then into egg mixture, then back into the bread crumbs. Press down on cutlet to ensure bread crumbs stick nicely. Then carefully place chicken in frying pan, and let fry approx. 5-6 on each side until cutlet is golden brown. Fry chicken in batches, place chicken in between paper towels in a large pan.

Chicken In Mushroom Sauce

23-pound chickens, quartered
2 to 3 Tbsps. Oil
1 large onion, diced
4 sprigs parsley, chopped
1 cup sliced mushrooms
¼ tsp.salt
¼ tsp. white pepper
2 cloves garlic, minced
2 Tbsps. Of flour
2 cups Tokay wine
2 lemons

Rinse chickens, remove excess fat, and pat dry.

In large pan heat oil over medium heat and saute the onions, then add parsley, mushrooms, salt, pepper and garlic.Simmer over low heat for 10-15 minutes.Stir in flour and mix well.Add the wine.Cook and stir the mixture until thickened.

Preheat the oven to 350°.Place chicken in large roasting pan, pour the sauce over the chicken.Bake covered for 1 hour, then remove cover and cook for an additional half hour.Squeeze fresh lemon juice over chicken when still warm.

Chicken Dumplings

2 whole chicken breasts, ground (approx. 1-2 lbs ground chicken)
1 onion grated
¼ cup bread crumbs or matzah meal
Pinch of salt
Pinch of pepper
1 egg beaten
STOCK:
8 cups of water
1 carrot, sliced
1 onion, sliced
1 parsley root
Dash of salt
Dash of pepper
Dash of sugar

In a medium bowl combine ground chicken, with onion, bread crumbs, salt, pepper and egg. Form mixture into small balls.

STOCK: In a 3 quart pot, boil the water with the carrot, onion, parsley root, salt, pepper and sugar. Bring to a rapid boil and add the chicken balls. Simmer, covered on low flame for 1 ½ hours.

Glazed Chicken

8 chicken drumsticks (about 2 lbs)

Salt, to taste

Ground black pepper, to taste

Garlic powder, to taste

Onion powder, to taste

1 (12 ounce) jar of apricot jam

¼ cup teriyaki sauce

1 Tbsp. brown sugar

1 tsp. cornstarch

1 tsp. apple cider vinegar

Preheat oven to 350°.Wash chicken and pat dry, place in 9x13 baking dish.Season the chicken with the salt, pepper, garlic and onion powders.Bake the chicken covered for 45 minutes.

Mix apricot jam, teriyaki sauce, brown sugar, cornstarch and apple cider vinegar in a small bowl.Remove chicken from the oven, pour the sauce over the chicken.Bake uncovered until chicken is tender and no longer pink, another 45 minutes.

Meat

Peppered Roast

1 (5 lb.) French roast
Salt, to taste
Ground black pepper, to taste
Garlic powder, to taste
Onion powder, to taste
Paprika
1 (10 oz.) bottle light horseradish sauce (golds)
1 (4.2 oz) spice bottle of whole black peppercorns

Preheat the oven to 350°. Rinse, and then pat meat dry. Place the meat into a 9x13 pan. Season the meat with all the spices. Spread the light horseradish sauce evenly over the roast. Place whole peppercorns over horseradish sauce, press down so peppercorns stick nicely.

Bake for 1 hour uncovered, roast between 1 hour and 1 hour and 15 minutes for medium rare, for well done back 1 ½ hours to 2 hours. Remove from oven and let meat rest for 15 minutes. When meat is cooled slice in thin slices, against the grain.

Hungarian Beef Goulash

3 Tbsps. Of oil
1 ½ cups chopped onion
1 small green pepper, finely diced
1 large clove garlic, minced
2 pounds stew meat, cut into ¾ inch cubes
6 cups water
2 Tbsps. Paprika
4 tsps. Salt
¼ tsp. cayenne pepper
1 ½ pounds potatoes, diced
1 16 oz. can whole tomatoes, sliced with liquid

Using a 5-quart Dutch oven, heat the oil, over low heat sauté the onion, green pepper, and garlic for 10 minutes or until tender.Add meat and brown.Add water and spices.Bring to a boil, lower the flame, cover and simmer for 1 ½ hours.

Add potatoes and cook covered 15 minutes, or until tender.Stir in tomatoes with the liquid and heat for another couple of minutes.

Honey Brisket

2 ½- 3 pound, beef brisket
SAUCE:
½ cup of ketchup
¼ cup of soy sauce
1/2 cup of honey
4 cloves of fresh garlic, chopped
1 onion, sliced
¼ cup of onion soup mix
1 ½ cups of water

Preheat the oven to 350 °. Placed sliced onions on bottom of a 9x13 baking pan.Rinse and place the brisket on top of the onion.Mix the rest of the ingredients in medium bowl until well blended.Pour the sauce over the brisket, cover and cook for 2 hours and 45 minutes.Remove from oven and let meat rest for 30 minutes.Then slice the roast thin, against the grain.Return the sliced meat to the pan and heat an additional 10 minutes.Serve and enjoy!

Veal Stew

½ cup of flour

1 tsp. of onion powder

1 tsp. of garlic powder

1 tsp. of salt

1 tsp. of paprika

2 pounds veal stew meat, cut into 1 ½ inch chunks

3 Tbsps. Oil

1 large onion, sliced

2 cloves garlic, minced

1 cup sliced mushrooms

3 potatoes peeled and cubed

2 peeled carrots, sliced

½ small green pepper, diced

2 tomatoes, diced

1 stalk of celery, diced

2 cups dry red wine

1 tsp. of thyme

1/8 tsp. curry powder

2 Tbsps. Soy sauce

1 tsp. salt

½ tsp. pepper

Mix flour, onion powder, garlic powder, salt and paprika in a large bowl.Toss the veal in flour mixture until well coated.In a large stock pot, brown the veal pieces in oil then remove from the pot.Add the onion, garlic and mushrooms to the oil and sauté for 10 minutes.Return the veal to the pot and add the potatoes, carrots, green peppers, tomatoes and celery. Add the wine and seasonings. Bring pot to a boil, lower heat and simmer for 2 hours until meat is tender.

Desserts

Amazing Chiffon Cake

7 eggs, separated
Pinch of salt
1 ½ cups of sugar
2 ¼ cups of flour
3 tsps. Baking powder
¾ cup apple juice, or orange juice, or water
2 tsps. Vanilla extract
½ cup oil
½ tsp. almond extract (optional)

Preheat oven to 350°. Beat egg whites and salt in large mixing bowl on high speed until peaks form. Gradually add ½ cup sugar, 1 tablespoon at a time, beating until stiff but not dry.
Set aside.

In a separate bowl, beat egg yolks, remaining sugar, and other ingredients well. Fold whites into egg yolk mixture with a rubber spatula and gently combine well.

Pour into an ungreased 10-inch tube pan and bake for 1 hour. When done, immediately invert pan on top of soda botle. Cool at least 3 hours before removing, when cool loosen edges and remove the cake from the pan.

Flaky Apricot Rugelach

2 Cups margarine, softened
110 ounce container nondairy dessert topping
5 ½- 6 ½ cups of flour
FILLING:
2 cups of apricot jam

In a large mixer bowl, cream margarine. Add dessert topping and then flour.Mix until dough is formed.Cover and refrigerate 4 hours or overnight.

Divide dough into six portions.

To fill and shape Rugelach:

1. On lightly floured surface roll out dough to approximately 1/8 inch thick circle.Brush a light coat of oil over the dough circle.Spread the filling over the oil leaving a ½ inch margin around the edge and in the middle of the dough.Cut the circle into 12-18 triangles depending how big you want each rugelach.

2. Roll each individual triangle, roll from wide outer edge inward to form a roll.Gently bend both ends toward center to form a crescent.

3. Brush each rugelach with beaten egg to glaze.

Preheat oven to 350°.Place rugelach on lightly greased cookie sheet and back approx. 30 minutes until lightly brown.

Chocolate Mousse Cake

1 stick margarine

7 eggs, separated

7 ounces chocolate chips

1 cup sugar

1 Tbsp. vanilla extract

1 carton dessert whip

4 Tbsps. Confectioners' sugar

Beat egg whites with ¼ cup sugar, set aside.

In a small saucepan, melt chocolate chips and margarine, let cool. Beat yolks with remaining sugar and vanilla. Add chocolate chip mixture to yolk mixture and mix well. Fold in egg whites. Pour ½ of mixture into greased tube pan. Bake for 30 minutes at 350°. Refrigerate remaining half of mixture. When cake is cooled, pour onto it refrigerated mixture and freeze for a few hours.

Beat dessert whip and sugar. Remove cake from pan and frost sides and top with dessert whip. Sprinkle with chocolate sprinkles and replace in freezer until a few minutes before serving.

Spiced Coffee Cake

½ cup margarine, softened

½ cup of sugar

½ cup of brown sugar

2 eggs

1 ¾ cups of flour

1 ½ tsps. Baking powder

1 tsp. salt

½ tsp. cinnamon

½ tsp. cloves

½ tsp. nutmeg

½ cup strong coffee, cooled

½ cup of raisins

Preheat oven to 350°.In a large bowl, cream together margarine and both sugars.Beat in eggs, one at a time.Add flour, baking powder, salt, cinnamon, cloves, nutmeg and coffee.Dust raisins lightly with flour, then add to rest of mixture.Pour into greased 9x13 pan.Bake for 25-30 minutes until done.Cool cake before removing from pan.0

Low Carb Zucchini Tomato Salad

Prep Time: 20 minutes*

Servings: 2

INGREDIENTS

1 medium zucchini

1 tomato

5 sundried tomatoes

1 garlic clove

2 fresh basil leaves

1 tablespoon raw virgin coconut oil (or 2 tablespoons warm water)

1/4 teaspoon ground white pepper (or black pepper)

1/4 teaspoon sea salt

INSTRUCTIONS

1. Run zucchini through spiralizer, slice into long, thin shreds with knife, or use vegetable peeler to make flat, thin slices. Sprinkle with a pinch of salt and pepper, and gently toss to coat.

2. Add tomato, sundried tomatoes, peeled garlic, basil, coconut oil or warm water, and remaining salt and pepper to food processor or bullet blender. Process until sauce of desired consistency forms.

3. Transfer zucchini pasta to serving bowls. Top with tomato sauce and serve immediately.

4. Or refrigerate for 20 minutes and serve chilled.

Easy Tomato Bisque

Prep Time: 5 minutes*

Servings: 2

Ingredients

3 plum tomatoes (1 cup roughly chopped)

1 sundried tomato

1 clove garlic

2 large basil leaves

1/4 cup raw cashews

3/4 cup water

1/2 teaspoon sea salt

1/4 teaspoon ground white pepper (or ground black pepper)

INSTRUCTIONS

1. *Soak cashews for 4 hours, then drain and rinse, if preferred.
2. Add all ingredients to high-speed blender and process until smooth, about 2 minutes.
3. Pour into serving bowl and serve immediately.

Spicy Kelp Noodle Salsa & Cashew Sauce

Prep Time: 10 minutes*

Servings: 2

INGREDIENTS

1 package (12 oz) kelp noodles

1/2 lemon

1 small red bell pepper

1 small carrot

Small bunch basil leaves
Crunchy Cashew Sauce

1 cup raw cashews

1 orange

1/2 lemon

1/2 teaspoon paprika

1/2 teaspoon ground oregano

1/2 teaspoon ground black pepper

1/2 teaspoon sea salt

INSTRUCTIONS

1.*Soak 3/4 cup cashews in enough water to cover at least 4 hours. Drain and rinse.

2.Rinse and drain kelp noodles. Add to medium bowl and soak 5 minutes in warm water and juice of 1/2 lemon.

3.Cut bell pepper in half, then remove stem, seeds and veins. Thinly slice bell pepper lengthwise. Use vegetable peeler or grater to make long, thin slices of carrot. Add veggies to medium mixing bowl.

4.For Crunchy Cashew Sauce, add soaked cashews, juice of lemon and orange, salt and spices to food processor or bullet. Process until very smooth.

5.Add drained kelp noodles to mixing bowl. Pour Crunchy cashew Sauce over veggies and kelp noodles. Chiffon basil leaves and chop remaining unsoaked cashews. Sprinkle over bowl.
6.Toss to coat. Transfer to serving dishes and serve immediately.
7.Or refrigerate for 20 minutes and serve chilled.

Raw Almond & Paprika

Prep Time: 15 minutes*

Servings: 2

Ingredients

1 cup raw almonds*

1/4 cup water

2 tablespoons coconut oil

1 tablespoon lemon juice

1 tablespoon raw apple cider vinegar

1 garlic clove

1/4 teaspoon paprika

1/4 teaspoon ground black pepper

1/2 teaspoon sea salt

4 - 6 sheets dried nori (seaweed paper)

INSTRUCTIONS

1.*For Almond Cheese, soak almonds in enough water to cover overnight. Drain and rinse. Pop off skins and discard.

2.Add soaked almonds, water, coconut oil, lemon juice, vinegar, peeled garlic, salt and spices to food processor or bullet blender and process until smooth. Add a few extra tablespoons of water if necessary to achieve thick but smooth consistency. Transfer Almond Cheese to serving dish.

3.Cut noriinto small sheets and serve with Almond Cheese.

Sweet Cabbage Avocado Slaw

Prep Time: 10 minutes*

Cook Time: 20 minutes

Servings: 4

INGREDIENTS

1/2 head cabbage (2 cups shredded)

1 avocado

1 carrot

Zest of 1 lemon

Juice of 1 lemon

1 tablespoon raw honey

2 tablespoons apple cider vinegar

1 teaspoon ground white pepper (or black pepper)

1 teaspoon sea salt

INSTRUCTIONS

1. Cut avocado in half and remove pit. Scoop flesh into large mixing bowl and mash with fork.
2. Remove any tough outer leaves and core from cabbage. Shred cabbage and carrot. Add to bowl with vinegar, honey, salt and pepper. Zest then juice lemon, and add.
3. Toss to combine.
4. Serve immediately. Or and place in refrigerator for 20 minutes and serve chilled.

Pink Fresh Coconut Shake

Prep Time: 5 minutes*

Cook Time: 0 minutes

Servings: 1
Ingredients

1 banana

1 cup strawberries

1/2 - 1 cup water

Meat of 1/2 fresh coconut (or 1/2 cup unsweetened flaked or shredded coconut)

INSTRUCTIONS
1. *Soak flaked coconut in water for at least 4 hours.
2. Add fresh or soaked flaked coconut and water to high-speed blender. Process on high until smooth, about 1 minute.
3. Strain coconut mixture through nut milk bag or a few layers of cheese cloth. Squeeze out all excess liquid. Reserve coconut milk. Dry excess coconut, process until finely ground, and use as coconut flour.
4. Remove leaves from strawberries and chop. Peel banana.
5. Add coconut milk to blender with fruit and process on high until smooth.
6. Pour into serving glass and serve immediately.
7. Or chill in refrigerator for 20 minutes, blend for a few seconds to incorporate separated liquid, then pour into serving glass and serve chilled.

Celery With Pitted Dates

Prep Time: 5 minutes

Servings: 2

INGREDIENTS

3 celery stalks

2 tablespoons dried cranberries
Cashew Butter

1 cup cashews

1 dried pitted date

1 teaspoon raw virgin coconut oil

1/2 teaspoon ground cinnamon

1/4 teaspoon sea salt

INSTRUCTIONS
1.Add cashews, date, cinnamon, salt and coconut oil to food processor or bullet blender. Process until smooth. Let mixture rest between periods of processing to reach desired consistency, if necessary.
2.Cut celery stalks into thirds and fill wells with Cashew Butter. Place cranberries on cashew butter.
3.Serve room temperature. Or refrigerate 10 minutes and serve chilled.

Vanilla Blueberry Energy Bars

Prep Time: 25 minutes

Servings: 6

Ingredients

1 cup dried blueberries

1/4 cup dried pitted dates

1/2 cup raw cashews

3/4 cup raw almonds

1/4 teaspoon ground cinnamon

1/4 teaspoon vanilla

Pinch sea salt

1/3 cup warm water

1 lemon

Instructions

1. Soak dried blueberries and dates in warm water and lemon juice for 5 - 10 minutes.
2. Add nuts to food processor or high-speed blender. Line loaf pan with parchment paper.
3. Drain fruit and add to processor with spices and pinch of lemon zest. Process for about 1 minute, until fruit and nuts break down and the mixture sticks together when pressed.
4. Scrape mixture into prepared loaf pan and press firmly into bottom with hands or spatula.
5. Place in refrigerator and chill for 10 minutes. Remove and cut into 6 bars.
6. Serve immediately. Or store in refrigerator up to 2 weeks.

Sweet Vanilla Peaches

Prep Time: 5 minutes

Servings: 2

INGREDIENTS

2 ripe peaches

1/4 cup raw honey

Pinch vanilla (optional)

Pinch cinnamon (optional)
Instructions

1.Add honey to small mixing bowl with optional spices. Beat with hand mixer or whisk until opaque, thick and creamy, about 5 - 10 minutes.

2.Cut peaches in half and remove pits. Slice peaches into wedges and arrange on serving dish. Transfer honey cream to serving bowl.

3.Serve immediately.

Raw Hazelnut Fudge

Prep Time: 10* minutes

Servings: 6

INGREDIENTS

1/4 cup raw cacao powder

3/4 cup raw almonds

1/2 cup raw hazelnuts (or cashews)

2 tablespoons raw virgin coconut oil

1/4 cup raw honey

1/4 cup hazelnuts (or walnuts)

Instructions

1. Line square baking dish with parchment paper.
2. Process almonds, 1/2 cup hazelnuts and coconut oil in food processor or bullet blender. Blend until fairly smooth and creamy.
3. Add nut butter, cocoa powder and honey to medium mixing bowl and mix well.
4. Chop remaining nuts.
5. *Spread mixture into parchment lined baking dish and top with chopped nuts. Refrigerate for 2 - 3 hours, until completely set.
6. Slice and serve chilled or room temperature.

Ginger Apricot Cookies

Prep Time: 20 minutes*

Servings: 12

INGREDIENTS

3/4 cup dried apricots (1/2 cup chopped)

3/4 cup dried pitted dates (1/2 cup chopped)

1/2 cup raw macadamia nuts (frozen)

2 inch piece fresh ginger

1 teaspoon ground ginger

1/4 teaspoon ground cinnamon

1/2 cup unsweetened flakes or shredded coconut

INSTRUCTIONS

1.* Place macadamia nuts in freezer for a few hours to overnight.

2. Add frozen nuts to food processor or high-speed blender. Pulse until coarsely ground.

3. Peel and finely grate fresh ginger. Add to processor with apricots, dates, ground ginger and cinnamon. Process until mixture is well broken down and sticks together.

4. Form the mixture into 12 balls and press flat. Roll cookies in coconut until well coated.

5. Cover and place in freezer for at least 10 minutes, until set up and firm.

6. Serve chilled.

7. Cover and store refrigerator or freezer until ready to serve.

Cauliflower Shrimp Mussels

Prep Time: 10 minutes

Cook Time: 25 minutes

Servings: 4

INGREDIENTS

1 large head cauliflower

8 oz chorizo (or other smoked sausage)

8 oz large shrimp

12 live little neck clams

12 live mussels

4 bone-in chicken thighs

1 cup chicken stock (or seafood stock)

1 small white onion

2 tablespoons smoked paprika

1 teaspoon saffron

Pinch ground black pepper

Pinch sea salt

2 tablespoons coconut oil

Instructions

1. Heat large pan over medium heat and add coconut oil.
2. Peel and chop onion. Add to hot oiled pan and sauté until translucent, about 2 minutes.
3. Add chicken thighs and brown about 5 minutes. Turn chicken over and cook another 5 minutes.
4. Rinse and clean clams and mussels, and remove any beards with pliers. Peel and devein shrimp. Cut chorizo into 1 inch slices. Set aside.

5.Roughly chop cauliflower and add to food processor with shredding attachment, process to "rice." Or mince cauliflower with knife.

6.Add riced or minced cauliflower to chicken and sauté 2 minutes. Add chorizo, clams, mussels and shrimp. Add paprika and saffron and sauté another 2 minutes.

7.Add chicken or seafood stock and stir to combine. Increase heat to high and bring to simmer. Reduce heat to medium-high and cover. Let simmer about 5- 7 minutes, until liquid evaporates, shrimp is opaque, and mussels and clams open. Discard any that do not open.

8.Plate and serve hot.

Easy Vanilla Chocó Soufflé

Prep Time: 10 minutes
Cook Time: 20 minutes
Servings: 2
Ingredients

2 eggs

3 oz organic chocolate (semisweet or bittersweet)

2 tablespoons cocoa powder

2 tablespoons sweetener*

2 tablespoons ghee (or cacao butter)

1 teaspoon vanilla

1/4 teaspoon sea salt

1/4 teaspoon cream of tartar

1 tablespoon ghee (or cacao butter)
Instructions

1. Preheat oven to 375 degrees F. Grease two 8oz ceramic ramekins with 1 tablespoon ghee or cacao butter. Coat ramekins with the cocoa, and tap out excess.
2. Melt chocolate and 2 tablespoons ghee or cacao butter in large bowl over double boiler, stirring occasionally.
3. Remove chocolate mixture from heat. Add egg whites to separate medium mixing bowl, and yolks to chocolate. Whisk yolks and vanilla into chocolate until smooth. Set aside.
4. Beat egg whites, sweetener, salt and cream of tartar with hand mixer or whisk until stiff peaks form, about 8 minutes.
5. Gently fold the egg-white mixture into the chocolate mixture. Spoon batter into prepared ramekins.
6. Place in oven and bake until risen and set, about 20 minutes.
7. Remove from oven and let cool slightly. Or turn off oven and crack door open to cool slowly.

8.Serve warm.
*Stevia, agave nectar or raw honey

Eggs With Smoked Salmon

Prep Time: 15 minutes
Cook Time: 25 minutes
Servings: 4
Ingredients

4 cage free eggs

6 oz smoked salmon

2 sprigs fresh dill
English Muffins

1/3 cup coconut flour

1/3 cup almond flour

2 eggs

1/4 cup almond milk (or low-fat coconut milk)

2 tablespoons coconut oil

1/2 teaspoon baking soda

1 teaspoon apple cider vinegar
Hollandaise Sauce

1/2 cup ghee or coconut oil (melted)

2 egg yolks

1/2 lemon

1/4 teaspoon sea salt

INSTRUCTIONS

1. Preheat oven to 400 degrees F. Coat 2 mini-round cake pans or 4-inch diameter ceramic ramekins with coconut oil. Bring medium pot to simmer with 1 teaspoon salt and 1 teaspoon apple cider vinegar.
2. For English Muffins, mix baking soda and apple cider vinegar In small bowl. Set aside and allow to froth.

3. In medium mixing bowl, beat egg whites with hand mixer or whisk until thick and frothy. Add yolks, almond and coconut flour, nut milk, and coconut oil. Mix gently.

4. Add baking soda and vinegar mixture to bowl and blend well until smooth and free of clumps.

5. Pour batter into pans or ramekins and place on sheet pan. Place in oven and bake 15 -18 minutes, until golden brown and center is firm to the touch.

6. Crack eggs into 4 separate small bowls. Coat or spray metal ladle with coconut oil. Hold ladle over simmering water and pour 1 egg into coated ladle. Slowly tilt edge of ladle into hot water, filling it gently while keeping ladle just submerged in water. Do not let egg float out of ladle or submerge ladle into water entirely. Hold and cook egg about 1 - 2 minutes, until whites are opaque and yolk is warmed but still runny. Place poached egg on paper towel to drain. Repeat with remaining eggs.

7. Remove muffins from oven. Loosen from sides of cake pans or ramekins with knife and turn out onto wire rack to cool.

8. For Hollandaise Sauce, add egg yolks, squeeze of lemon, and salt to food processor or high-speed blender. Processor for 30 seconds. While processor or blender is running, drizzle in melted ghee or coconut oil very slowly. Process until all fat is added and emulsified and sauce thickens a bit, about 2 minutes.

9. Cut slightly cool English Muffins in half and transfer to serving dish.

10. Layer English Muffin halves with smoked salmon, then top with a poached egg. Pour Hollandaise Sauce over poached eggs, to taste. Sprinkle with pinch of salt and cracked black pepper, if preferred. Chop dill and sprinkle over eggs.

11. Serve immediately.

Pink Chia Creamy Bread

Prep Time: 10 minutes
Cook Time: 10 minutes
Servings: 12- 16
INGREDIENTS
1 cup coconut flour
3/4 cup cashew flour (or almond flour)
1/4 cup ground chia seed (or flax meal)
1/2 cup coconut oil
2 eggs
1/4 cup coconut crème
1/4 cup sweetener*
1/4 cup unsweetened apple sauce
1 teaspoons baking powder
1tablespoon ground cinnamon
1 teaspoon ground ginger
1 teaspoon ground white pepper (or black pepper)
1 teaspoon sea salt
2 cups fresh sliced strawberries
1/2 cup chopped walnuts (optional)
Instructions

1.Preheat oven to 350 degrees F.Line muffin pan with paper liners or coat with coconut oil.
2.In large bowl, whisk eggs with hand mixer or whisk until frothy and light. Add coconut oil, sweetener and applesauce. Blend until combined. Slice strawberries, and fold in with walnuts (optional).

3.Inmedium bowl, blend flours, chia meal, baking powder, salt and spices.Stir flour blend into strawberry mixture until well combined.

4.Use ice cream scoop or tablespoon to scoop equal portions of batter into muffin pans, 1/2 - 3/4 full. Line or oil more muffin pans if excess batter remains.

5.Bake for 15 minutes, or until golden brown and firm but springy to the touch.

6.Cool enough to handle. Serve warm or room temperature.

NOTE: Bake in square oiled baking pan for 25 - 35 minutes or two oiled loaf pans for 35 - 45 minutes for **Strawberry Loaves**.

*stevia, raw honey or agave nectar

Almond With Apple Sauce – A Low Carb Morning Dish

Prep Time: 10 minutes

Cook Time: 20 minutes

Servings: 24

INGREDIENTS

2 cups coconut flour

1 cup almond flour

12 ounces organic hard cider

2 eggs

1/2 cup unsweetened applesauce

1 tart apple

2 tablespoons baking powder

1 teaspoon ground nutmeg

1 teaspoon ground black pepper

1 teaspoon sea salt

Instructions

1. Preheat oven to 375 degrees F. Line 2 muffin pans with paper liners or coat with coconut oil.
2. Peel, core and grate or dice apple, and place in large bowl. Pour hard apple cider over apples, plus nutmeg and black pepper.
3. In medium bowl, whisk eggs with hand mixer or whisk until frothy and light. Add applesauce and blend until combined. Add egg mixture to cider and apples.
4. Slowly sift and stir flours, baking powder and salt into wet ingredients.
5. Use ice cream scoop or tablespoon to scoop equal portions of batter into muffin pans, 1/2 - 3/4 full.

6.Bake for 15 - 20 minutes, or until golden brown and firm but springy to the touch.

7.Cool enough to handle. Serve warm or room temperature.

NOTE: Bake in square oiled baking pan for 35 - 45 minutes or two oiled loaf pans for 45 - 55 minutes for **Apple Cider Loaves**.

*stevia, raw honey or agave nectar

No Grain Low Carb Almond Bread

Prep Time: 5 minutes
Cook Time: 20 minutes
Servings: 8

INGREDIENTS

2 cups almond flour
2 tablespoons ground chia seed (or flax meal)
2 eggs
1/2 cup unsweetened applesauce
1/4 cup coconut oil
1/4 cup sweetener*
1 tablespoon baking powder
1 teaspoon baking soda
2 tablespoons ground ginger
1 tablespoon vanilla
1 tablespoon ground cinnamon
1 teaspoon ground black pepper
1/2 teaspoon ground cloves
1/2 teaspoon cardamom (optional)
1 oz fresh ginger juice (optional)

Instructions

1. Preheat oven to 350 degrees F. Coat 2 small loaf pans with coconut oil.
2. In large bowl, beat eggs until light and thickened. Add applesauce, oil, sweetener and ginger juice (optional). Beat well.
3. In medium bowl, blendall dry ingredients well. Slowly stir flour mixture into egg mixture.
4. Pour batter into loaf pans and bake for 20 - 25 minutes, or until toothpick inserted into center comes out clean.

5.Let cool slightly. Insert knife around edges and remove from pan. Serve warm or room temperature.

NOTE: Bake in large oiled loaf pan for 35 - 45 minutes for **Grain-Free Gingerbread Loaf**.

* raw honey, agave nectar, grade B maple syrup, molasses

Low Carb Almond Corn Muffins

Prep Time: 5 minutes

Cook Time: 15 minutes

Servings: 12

Ingredients

1 cup almond flour

2 eggs

1/4 cup coconut oil

2 tablespoons unsweetened applesauce

1 teaspoon sweetener*

1 teaspoon organic apple cider vinegar

1 teaspoon baking powder

1/2 teaspoon ground turmeric (optional)

Pinch ground white pepper (optional)

INSTRUCTIONS
1. Preheat oven to 350 degrees F. Line muffin pan with paper liners or lightly coat with coconut oil.
2. Beat eggs in medium mixing bowl with hand mixer or whisk until thick and slightly frothy. Add oil, applesauce, sweetener, and vinegar and mix well.
3. Stir in almond meal, baking powder, and turmeric and white pepper (optional) until combined.
4. Use ice cream scoop or tablespoon to scoop batter into muffin pan, about 1/2 - 3/4 full.
5. Bake 15 - 18 minutes until edges are golden brown and the tops are firm.
6. Serve warm or room temperature.

NOTE: Bake in square oiled baking pan for 25 - 35 minutes for **"Corn" Bread**.
*stevia, raw honey or agave nectar

Quick Delicious Almond Biscuits – Evening Snack

Prep Time: 5 minutes
Cook Time: 15 minutes
Servings: 8
Ingredients

2 1/2 cups fine ground almond flour

2 eggs

1/4 cup coconut oil

1 teaspoon baking soda

1/2 teaspoon sea salt

1 tablespoon sweetener*

INSTRUCTIONS
1. Preheat oven to 350 degrees F. Line sheet pan with parchment paper.
2. Combine almond flour, baking soda and salt in medium bowl.
3. Separate egg whites into separate medium bowl, and yolk into small bowl. Beat egg whites to soft peaks with hand mixer or whisk.
4. Mix yolks, oil and sweetener into whites. Mix wet ingredients into dry to form soft, solid dough.
5. Roll dough into eight (8) 1-inch thick round biscuits with hands. Place on parchment covered sheet pan and bake for 12 - 15 minutes, or until golden and firm on top. Serve warm.

NOTE: Oil square baking pan, gently press in dough, cut into 9 squares, and bake for 20 - 25 minutes for break-away pan biscuits.
*stevia, raw honey or agave nectar

Coconut & Almond Flour Fry Bread

Prep Time: 5 minutes

Cook Time: 15 minutes

Servings: 2
Ingredients

1 cup coconut flour

1 cup almond flour (or cashew flour)

1/4 cup tapioca flour/starch

3 eggs

1/2 cup coconut oil

1/2 cup full-fat coconut milk

1 teaspoon baking powder

2 tablespoons sweetener*

Pinch sea salt

Water (for thinning)

Coconut oil (for cooking)

INSTRUCTIONS

1. Heat medium skillet over medium-high heat and coat generously with coconut oil.
2. Blend eggs, oil, milk and sweetener in food processor or bullet blender until smooth and a bit airy.
3. In medium bowl, combine flours, baking powder and salt. Add egg mixture and combine to form soft dough. If too tough, add water 1 tablespoon at a time.
4. Form dough into 2 large flat rounds with hands. Place 1 round in pan and cook about 3 minutes, or until puffed and browned. Flip fry bread with tongs or spatula and cook another 3 minutes, or until golden and cooked through.
5. Repeat with remaining dough. Re-oil pan as necessary.
6. Drain hot fry bread on paper towel. Serve warm.

NOTE: For **BakedFry Bread** , generously coat two 9-inch round cake pans with coconut oil. Press dough into pansand brush tops with coconut oil. Bake at 425 degrees F infor 15 minutes, or until cooked through and golden.
*stevia, raw honey or agave nectar

Crunchy Coconut Crackers

Prep Time: 10 minutes

Cook Time: 10 minutes

Servings: 4
Ingredients

1 cup coconut flour

3/4 cup almond flour

4 egg whites

1/4 cup coconut oil

1/4 cup coconut crème

1/4 cup sweetener

1/2 cup flaked coconut

1 teaspoon vanilla

1/2 teaspoon baking soda

3/4 teaspoon sea salt

1/2 teaspoon ground white pepper (or black pepper)
Instructions

1.Preheat oven to 375 degrees F.Line sheet pan with parchment paper or coat with coconut oil. Prepare two additional sheets of parchment.

2.Whisk egg and oil with hand mixer or whisk until blended and slightly frothy. Add sweetener, coconut crème and vanilla,and continue blending.

3.Sift in half of flour, baking soda, vanilla,salt and pepper. Add coconut flakes. Sift in remaining flour.Stir and bring dough together.

4.Form dough into rectangle and flatten with hands on parchment. Cover with second sheet of parchment and flatten to about 1/4 inch with rolling pin. Remove top layer of parchment.

5.Cut rectangles from dough with pizza cutter or sharp knife. Carefully flip dough onto sheet pan. Arrange at least 1/2 inch apart on sheet pan.

6.Bake for about 10 minutes, or until crisp and golden brown. Remove and let cool. Serve room temperature.

Chocó Dip With Celery

Prep Time: 10 minutes*

Servings: 2

INGREDIENTS

2- 3 medium celery stalks
Hazelnut Spread

1 cup raw hazelnuts

1/4 cup raw cocoa powder

1/4 cup raw honey (or dried pitted dates)

1/2 teaspoon vanilla

Pinch Celtic sea salt

Raw nut milk (optional)

Water

INSTRUCTIONS

1.*Soak hazelnuts in enough water to cover overnight in refrigerator. Drain and rinse. Soak dates in enough water to cover overnight in refrigerator, if using. Drain.

2.Add soaked hazelnuts to food processor or high-speed blender and process until smooth, up to 10 minutes. Scrape down sides as needed.

3.Add honey or soaked dates, cocoa powder, vanilla and salt to processor. Process until smooth, about 1minute. Add nut milk to reach desired consistency (optional).

4.Cut celery stalks into 3 in pieces. Scoop Hazelnut Spread into wells of celery with small spoon or knife. Fill wells completely and smooth with knife or back of spoon. Transfer filled celery to serving dish.

5.Serve immediately. Or refrigerate 20 minutes and serve chilled.

Chocó Pecan Snack

Prep Time: 10 minutes*

Servings: 6

INGREDIENTS

1 cup raw pecans

1 cup dried pitted dates

2 tablespoons raw coconut butter (or cacao butter)

1/4 cup raw cocoa powder

1/4 cup shredded or flaked coconut

1/4 teaspoon Celtic sea salt

Instructions

1. Line square baking dish with parchment paper. Allow coconut or cacao butter to soften.
2. Add pecans to food processor or high-speed blender and process until finely ground, about 1 minute.
3. Add dates and coconut or cacao butter and process until mixture sticks together, about 1 - 2 minutes.
4. Add cocoa, coconut and salt. Process until well ground but not completely smooth.
5. *Transfer mixture to parchment lined baking dish and firmly press into bottom with hands or spatula. Refrigerate until set, about 2 hours.
6. Remove from refrigerator. Slice and serve chilled. Or allow to warm to room temperature and serve.

Vanilla Chocó Chip Cookies

Prep Time: 35 minutes

Servings: 6

INGREDIENTS

1 1/4 cups fine almond flour

3 teaspoons coconut flour

1/3 cup dried pitted dates

1/4 cup raw coconut butter (or cacao butter)

1 teaspoon vanilla

1/8 teaspoon Celtic sea salt

1/2 cup raw chocolate chips (or chopped raw chocolate bark or cacao nibs)

Instructions

1. Allow coconut or cacao butter to soften at room temperature. Line sheet pan with parchment paper.
2. Add softened butter and dates to food processor or high speed blender. Process until fairly smooth, about 2 minutes.
3. Add half of almond and coconut flours, and process for about 1 minute. Add remaining flour, vanilla and salt. Process until mixture comes together. Stir in chocolate or cacao nibs.
4. Use tablespoon or mini ice cream scoop to form dough into balls. Set on lined sheet pan and place in refrigerator 30 minutes.
5. Remove from refrigerator and serve chilled. Or allow to warm slightly and serve room temperature.

Sugar-Free Coconut Ice Cream

Prep Time: 30 minutes*

Servings: 4

Ingredients

2 1/2 cups shredded or flaked coconut (or 3 mature coconuts + 1/2 cups shredded or flaked coconut)

3/4 cup dried pitted dates (or raw honey)

1 1/2 teaspoons vanilla

Water

INSTRUCTIONS

1. *Freeze ice cream maker canister for at least 12 hours.
2. *Soak 2 cups coconut in 4 cups water at least 6 hours, or overnight in refrigerator. Soak dates in enough water to cover at least 6 hours, or overnight in refrigerator (if using). Drain.
3. Add soaked coconut, soaking liquid and dates (if using) to food processor or high-speed blender.
4. Or remove flesh from fresh coconuts and add to high-speed blender with 4 cups water and dates (if using). Process until well blended and fairly smooth, about 1 - 2 minutes.
5. Strain mixture through nut milk bag, cheesecloth or strainer back into blender. Reserve pulp and set aside to dry and dehydrate, then use as coconut flour.
6. Add 1/2 cup shredded or flaked coconut, vanilla and honey (if using) to coconut milk. Process to combine, about 10 seconds.
7. Assemble ice cream maker and turn on. Slowly pour mixture into running ice cream maker. Let machine run for about 20 minutes, until ice cream is set.
8. Transfer to serving dish and serve immediately.

www.ingramcontent.com/pod-product-compliance
Lightning Source LLC
Chambersburg PA
CBHW071439070526
44578CB00001B/152